Ramya Nagesh is a practising barrister at No5 Chambers. She acts in the full range of criminal matters, from the sublime to the ridiculous and everything in between. She is particularly interested in issues that raise complex and novel points of law and practice. The topic of Insane and Non-Insane Automatism does not disappoint. As a result of her keen interest and research in this area over the last nine years, she has written articles in peer-reviewed criminal law journals and continues to deliver seminars on the subject.

Ramya has written two other books on the subject of criminal law: *A Practical Guide to the Law In Relation to Hate Crime* and *Covid-19 and the Criminal Law: an Essential Guide*.

A Practical Guide to Insane and Non-Insane Automatism in Criminal Law

Sleepwalking, Blackouts, Hypoglycaemia, and Other Issues

A Practical Guide to Insane and Non-Insane Automatism in Criminal Law

Sleepwalking, Blackouts, Hypoglycaemia, and Other Issues

Ramya Nagesh
Barrister (Lincoln's Inn),
LLB (Hons), MSc (LSE)

Law Brief Publishing

© Ramya Nagesh

All rights reserved. No part of this publication may be reproduced, stored in a retrieval system, or transmitted, in any form or by any means, electronic, mechanical, photocopying, recording or otherwise, without the prior permission of the publisher.

Excerpts from judgments and statutes are Crown copyright. Any Crown Copyright material is reproduced with the permission of the Controller of OPSI and the Queen's Printer for Scotland. Some quotations may be licensed under the terms of the Open Government Licence (http://www.nationalarchives.gov.uk/doc/open-government-licence/version/3).

Cover image © iStockphoto.com/BrianAJackson

The information in this book was believed to be correct at the time of writing. All content is for information purposes only and is not intended as legal advice. No liability is accepted by either the publisher or author for any errors or omissions (whether negligent or not) that it may contain. Professional advice should always be obtained before applying any information to particular circumstances.

Published 2021 by Law Brief Publishing, an imprint of Law Brief Publishing Ltd
30 The Parks
Minehead
Somerset
TA24 8BT

www.lawbriefpublishing.com

Paperback: 978-1-913715-89-2

PREFACE

Every so often a criminal practitioner is handed a case which raises a unique and even astonishing defence. The usual defences in any criminal case may be divided into three broad groups: factual denial, self-defence or mistaken identification. What, then, is the recourse when a defendant claims that they were sleepwalking at the time, were out of control during an epileptic fit or quite simply legally insane when they committed the relevant act?

It is those cases with which this book concerns itself. We must be under no illusions that they will form the 'bread and butter' of the criminal practitioner. They will not be the sort of cases that arise every day. However, they will be the sort of cases that raise unusual and fascinating issues. This is one of the few spaces in the criminal law where logic and common sense do not always accord with the legal doctrine. We see sleepwalkers classed as insane, people found guilty despite the fact that mind altering drugs destroyed their ability to make reasoned decisions and the diabetic's sanity status resting upon whether they had too much or too little insulin on the day in question.

The operation of the law in this area is not only intriguing but is also essential knowledge for any of us who practise within the criminal justice system. When that case does land on our desk, we should be able to handle it with the appropriate care and expertise.

I make clear that this book is very much concerned with the use of insane and non-insane automatism as defences in the criminal law. It is not, therefore, concerned with the situation where a person may be unfit to plead or face trial. That relates to the accused's mental state at the time of proceedings, whereas we are concerned with their mental state at the time of the offences. Whilst that is an interesting and useful topic in itself, it is best saved as a subject for another day.

Additionally, the law of diminished responsibility is relevant to the accused's mental state at the time of committing a killing, but does not raise the same quagmire of issues as the interplay between insane and non-insane automatism. For that reason, I include an overview of the law on diminished responsibility, but it will not form a central part of this book.

What this book will do is provide you with a thorough understanding of insane and non-insane automatism in the criminal justice system today. We will undertake separate analyses of those which I term 'special cases' – where the law does not always seem to accord with medical or common sense. I have chosen sleepwalking, epilepsy, diabetes, intoxication, pre-menstrual syndrome, psychological blows and undiagnosed sleep apnoea as the subjects of further study.

Following that, I will consider whether the current law is fit for purpose. There have been numerous calls for reform of the existing law. I consider that no study of insane and non-insane automatism would be complete without a discussion about how the law could be changed.

Finally, I include what I hope is a helpful checklist of practical tips for all practitioners dealing with a case of automatism.

The law within this book is up to date to the time of writing on 14 October 2021.

Ramya Nagesh
October 2021

CONTENTS

Chapter One	An Overview of Insane and Non-Insane Automatism	1
	Key Features of Insane Automatism	3
	Key Features of Non-Insane Automatism	3
Chapter Two	Insane Automatism	5
	A History of Insane Automatism	5
	Current Law: Approaches in the Crown and Magistrates' Courts	9
Chapter Three	Non-Insane Automatism	27
	What Does Non-Insane Automatism Mean?	27
	Guidance From the Courts	28
	Guidance From the Law Commission	32
Chapter Four	Diminished Responsibility – A Third Option	35
	Background to Diminished Responsibility	35
	The Current Legislation	36
	The Elements of The Offence	37
Chapter Five	Special Cases – Epilepsy	43
Chapter Six	Special Cases – Diabetes	47
Chapter Seven	Special Cases – Sleepwalking	53
Chapter Eight	Special Cases – Intoxication	61
Chapter Nine	Special Cases – Discrete Situations	71
	Pre-Menstrual Syndrome	71
	Undiagnosed Sleep Apnoea	72
	Psychological Blow	73

Chapter Ten	Scope for Reform?	75
Conclusion – Practical Tips		79
Bibliography		81

CHAPTER ONE

AN OVERVIEW OF INSANE AND NON-INSANE AUTOMATISM

Within the criminal law, we are often concerned with whether the accused actually committed the act with which they are charged. The accused may claim that a witness is mistaken, is lying or that someone prompted the accused to commit the act out of self-defence. The law of insane and non-insane automatism is concerned, however, with the accused's state of mind and ability to control themselves at the time. The accused in these cases will claim that they were not mentally responsible for what their body did.

The law draws a fundamental distinction between automatism caused by insanity, and that which is not.

It is important to remember, first, that the word 'insanity' in this context is very much a legal concept. It does not always correlate with what the medical community would term 'insanity'. The law has imposed a far broader definition: a defect of reason caused by a disease of the mind which renders the accused unable to know what they are doing or to appreciate that it is wrong.

One of the ways in which the law seeks to distinguish whether a condition is insane or non-insane automatism is to identify whether the cause of that automatism is an internal or external factor. Internal causes are said to be indicative of insane automatism. External causes are said to give rise to a defence of sane automatism.

A long-standing justification for such a distinction has been that internal causes are more likely to recur, and so the greater powers of disposal (as to which, see below) available after an insanity verdict would help prevent that. However, this argument is not always sustainable. For example, a sleepwalker is highly unlikely to commit violence whilst asleep. Having done so once, there is no medical evidence to indicate that the sleepwalker will be likely to commit violence again. Whilst sleepwalkers can be treated medically, they are often given lifestyle advice to control their somnambulism. It is difficult, then, to see why there would be greater justification to find that a sleepwalker was legally insane than to find that they were suffering from a form of non-insane automatism.

It is perhaps for this reason that the Court of Appeal in *Burgess* (1991) WLR 1206 moved away from the possibility of recurrence as a determinative factor at 1212:

> "*If there is a danger of recurrence that may be an added reason for categorising the condition as a disease of the mind. On the other hand the absence of the danger of recurrence is not a reason for saying that it cannot be a disease of the mind.*"

That is not to say that the 'internal'/'external' distinction is worthless. In cases at either end of the automatism spectrum we can see how it can be useful. A person suffering from a long-term mental illness that causes him to be unaware of his actions is undoubtedly driven by an internal factor. A person who has been so distracted by a swarm of bees in his car whilst driving, such that he crashes the car, is undoubtedly triggered by an external factor. However, the difficulty arises within the shades of grey between the extremes. For example, can it be said that a sleepwalker who commits a violent act whilst asleep is guided by an internal factor (his proclivity to sleepwalk) or the numerous external factors that may have triggered the somnambulism (such as caffeine or external disturbances to sleep)?

These questions are important ones. The decision as to whether a particular person's condition falls within insane or non-insane automatism has impact on the burden of proof at trial, and the outcome for the accused if the defence is successful.

We will delve into both in more detail. This chapter is merely a brief introduction to both concepts. With that in mind, I set out a quick reference guide to the key features of insane and non-insane automatism below.

KEY FEATURES OF INSANE AUTOMATISM

The key features of a defence of insane automatism are:

(i) The burden of proof is on the defence;

(ii) The standard of proof is the balance of probabilities;

(iii) The claim must be supported by the written or oral evidence of two or more registered medical practitioners, at least one of whom is 'duly approved' (section 1 of the Criminal Procedure (Insanity and Unfitness to Plead) Act 1991);

(iv) If the defence succeeds, there will be a special verdict of 'not guilty by reason of insanity'. The defendant will not necessarily walk free, however. He may be made the subject of a hospital order under section 5(2) of the Criminal Procedure (Insanity) Act 1964.

KEY FEATURES OF NON-INSANE AUTOMATISM

The key features of a defence of non-insane automatism are:

(i) The defendant bears only an evidential burden. Whilst merely raising the defence is not enough, he needs only to introduce such evidence as might leave a reasonable jury in reasonable doubt as to whether he was in the state alleged. It is then for the prosecution to disprove the defence to the usual criminal standard;

(ii) If the automatism is self-induced, the defendant's liability will turn on the principles relating to intoxication;

(iii) If the defence is successful – i.e. the prosecution cannot disprove automatism – the verdict will be one of outright acquittal. There will be no scope for hospital order or other form of detention.

CHAPTER TWO

INSANE AUTOMATISM

A HISTORY OF INSANE AUTOMATISM

For hundreds of years, insanity has been recognised as a legitimate defence to a criminal charge. In the 18th Century, there was Arnold's Case (1724) 16 St Tr 695, where the accused shot Lord Onslow and claimed that he was insane at the time, albeit unsuccessfully. At the turn of the 19th Century, Hadfield's Case (1800) 27 St Tr 1281 saw the accused acquitted on the grounds of insanity at his trial for the attempted assassination of King George III. The Criminal Lunatics Act 1800 provided for a 'special verdict' of acquittal by reason of insanity, with an order for custody during His Majesty's Pleasure. Despite these cases, though, the law in relation to insanity was far from clear for many years.

That was to change by virtue of a series of events in 1843. During the afternoon of 20 January 1843, civil servant Edward Drummond was walking towards Downing Street from Charing Cross when he was shot in the back at point blank range. The shooter was Daniel M'Naghten, a Scottish woodturner. In the years preceding the shooting, M'Naghten had complained to a number of people that he was being persecuted by the Conservative Party and was shadowed by their spies. It is generally believed that in shooting Mr Drummond, he believed that he was shooting the man's employer, the Prime Minister.

When Mr Drummond died from his wounds five days later, M'Naghten faced trial for his murder. M'Naghten's defence was that at the time of the murder, he was suffering from delusions that amounted to insanity. Medical evidence was called on his behalf to show that he had not been in a sound state of mind, was suffering from morbid delusions, had no moral perception of right and wrong and was not capable of exercising control over his actions. The acquittal of M'Naghten for his murder was to lead to much controversy, which in turn led to arguably the most important statement of principles in the area of insane automatism.

The principles were borne after debate about the case in the House of Lords. Their Lordships made the decision to seek the advice of the Judges as to the state of the law, and submitted the following five questions to them:

(i) What is the law respecting alleged crimes committed by persons afflicted with insane delusion in respect of one or more particular subjects of persons: as, for instance, where at the time of the commission of the alleged crime the accused knew he was acting contrary to law, but did the act complained of with a view, under the influence of insane delusion, of redressing or revenging some supposed grievance or injury, or of producing some supposed public benefit?

(ii) What are the proper questions to be submitted to the jury, where a person alleged to be inflicted with insane delusion is charged with the commission of a crime and insanity is set up as a defence?

(iii) In what terms ought the question be left to the jury as to the accused's state of mind at the time when the act was committed?

(iv) If a person is under insane delusion as to existing facts, and commits an offence as a result, is he thereby excused?

(v) Can a medical man who is familiar with insanity, but never saw the accused before the trial, be asked his opinion as to the accused's state of mind at the time of the commission of the alleged offence?

The answers were, taking them in the same order as the questions to which they relate, *per* Tindal CJ:

(i) A person is guilty if he knew that he was acting contrary to law, notwithstanding that he was under the delusion that he was redressing or revenging a supposed grievance or injury, or producing some supposed public benefit;

(ii) And (iii) were taken together. The jury ought to be told in all cases that every man is presumed to be sane, and to possess a sufficient degree of reason to be responsible for his crimes, until the contrary is proved to their satisfaction. In order to be establish a defence on the ground of insanity, it must be clearly proved that, at the time of committing the act, the party accused was labouring under such a defect of reason, from disease of the mind, as not to know the nature and quality of the act he was doing, or, if he did know it, that he did not know he was doing what was wrong;

(iii) The answer to this was combined with the answer to question (ii) above;

(iv) The person labouring under a delusion must be considered in the same situation as to responsibility as if the facts with respect to which the delusion exists were real. For example, if he thinks that another man is trying to kill him, and he kills that person in 'self-defence', he would be exempt from punishment;

(v) The medical man who has no previous familiarity with the accused cannot strictly speaking be asked his opinion on whether the accused was insane at the time of the offence. That is because the questions to be answered are questions of fact for the jury to decide, rather than questions of pure science. However, where the facts are admitted or not disputed and the question is one of science only, it may be convenient to allow the question to be put in that general form to the witness, though the same cannot be insisted on as a matter of right.

The answers to these five questions became the 'M'Naghten Rules', which not only governed the courts' interpretations of the law in relation to insane automatism for years afterwards, but continue to do so today. It is the answer to questions (ii) and (iii) in particular which sets out the fundamental test to be applied:

> "*[A person is legally insane if] at the time of committing the act, the party accused was labouring under such a defect of reason, from disease of the mind, as not to know the nature and quality of the act he was doing, or, if he did know it, that he did not know he was doing what was wrong.*"

We will consider this test further within the next section in this chapter.

Of course, the mere opinions of judges outside of a courtroom setting are not, strictly speaking, a source of law. However around 140 years later, the House of Lords confirmed the legal status of the Rules in Sullivan (1983) 2 All ER 673, holding that they have provided a comprehensive definition since 1843. The M'Naghten Rules are undoubtedly binding law.

Around 40 years after the M'Naghten Rules, the Trial of Lunatics Act 1883 ("the 1883 Act") was enacted. Section 2 of the 1883 Act provided that the jury were to return a special verdict in cases where the accused's insanity defence was proven. This therefore distinguished a straightforward acquittal from that where the acquittal was on the grounds of insanity.

CURRENT LAW: APPROACHES IN THE CROWN AND MAGISTRATES' COURTS

Although the defence of insanity is available in both the Crown and the Magistrates' Courts, they are not governed by the same legal guidance. The Crown Court has the benefit of statute; the Magistrates' Court is far more heavily reliant on common law. It is worth arming ourselves with that knowledge before delving into a deeper analysis of the law of insane automatism.

THE CROWN COURT

We have seen that the modern law of insanity is still based upon the 19th Century M'Naghten Rules. Trials on Indictment have since been assisted by additional statutory guidance. Section 2 of the 1883 Act remains in force to this day. Its current iteration, following amendment by the Criminal Procedure (Insanity) Act 1964, is:

> *"2.— Special verdict where accused found guilty, but insane at date of act or omission charged, and orders thereupon.*
>
> *(1) Where in any indictment or information any act or omission is charged against any person as an offence, and it is given in evidence on the trial of such person for that offence that he was insane, so as not to be responsible, according to law, for his actions at the time when the act was done or omission made, then, if it appears to the jury before whom such person is tried that he did the act or made the omission charged, but was insane as aforesaid at the time when he did or made the same, the jury shall return [a special verdict that the accused is not guilty by reason of insanity."*

Section 1(1) of the Criminal Procedure (Insanity and Unfitness to Plead) Act 1991 sets out the following additional requirement:

> "*1.— Acquittals on grounds of insanity.*
>
> *(1) A jury shall not return a special verdict under section 2 of the Trial of Lunatics Act 1883 (acquittal on ground of insanity) except on the written or oral evidence of two or more registered medical practitioners at least one of whom is duly approved.*"

Section 1(2) of that Act states that the section 54(2) and (3) of the Mental Health Act 1983 (relating to the form that medical reports may take) apply equally to section 2 of the 1883 Act.

Section 5 of the Criminal Procedure (Insanity) Act 1964 provides that the Court shall make one of the following orders when there has been a special verdict:

(i) A hospital order (with or without a restriction order);

(ii) A supervision order;

(iii) An order for his absolute discharge.

Section 5(3) of the 1964 Act states that where the sentence for the offence in question is fixed by law and the Court has the power to make a hospital order, the Court shall make a hospital order with restrictions.

Section 5(3A) of the 1964 Act states that where the Court has the power to make an order for absolute discharge "*they may do so where they think, having regard to the circumstances, including the nature of the offence charged and the character of the accused, that such an order would be most suitable in all the circumstances of the case.*" An order for absolute discharge may well, therefore, be suitable in circumstances where the accused is of good or virtually good character, and the offence is not serious.

THE MAGISTRATES' COURT

It should not be forgotten that the defence of insanity is also available in the Magistrates' Courts. In *R (Singh) v Stratford Magistrates' Court* (2007) EWHC 1582 (Admin), the High Court considered the powers of the magistrates' court when faced with a defence of insanity. The Prosecution, first, submitted that the Magistrates' Court did not have jurisdiction to decide the issue of insanity. In rejecting that particular submission, the High Court held (at paragraph 14):

> "*I have no doubt that that argument is wrong. Insanity can be relied upon in the Magistrates' Court. If established, it prevents conviction. Whether it always entitles the accused to acquittal is another matter.*"

And at paragraph 22:

> "*There is no reason whatever why insanity should be excluded from the consideration of the Magistrates' court and every reason why it should not. It is a common law defence. If established by the accused in a case to which it is relevant, it prevents conviction.*"

The question then arises as to how procedure in the Magistrates' Court is governed. We have seen that the 1883 and 1991 Acts apply to the Crown Court only. The High Court in *Singh*, provides some assistance in this respect. It considered the ambit of the powers afforded to the Magistrates' Court under section 37 of the Mental Health Act 1983. Those are powers given to the Magistrates' Court to authorise the accused's admission to and detention in a hospital or under the guardianship of a social services authority (see sections 37(1) and 37(3) of the Act). At paragraph 25, the High Court concluded:

> "*25. Just as there is no statutory provision for a special verdict of not guilty by reason of insanity in a magistrates' court, so also there is no statutory procedure for the trial of the issue of fitness to plead. The plain statutory scheme is that section 37(3) is sufficiently flexible to*

cater for both situations (which may of course overlap) and, it may be, for others. The natural reading of section 37(3) is that it provides the magistrate with the power, in an appropriate case, to abstain from either convicting or acquitting, but instead to make a hospital or guardianship order."

Section 37(3) of the 1983 Act gives the Magistrates' Court the power to make a hospital or guardianship order without convicting him, so long as the Court is satisfied that he did the act with which he was charged. The effect is, then, that when faced with a defence of insanity, the Magistrates' Court need not formally convict or acquit. Instead a fact-finding exercise should take place, whether by virtue of admissions or hearing evidence (paragraph 35 of *Singh*). The Magistrates' Court is only compelled to proceed to trial where it is clear on the medical evidence that no order under section 37(3) of the 1983 Act is going to be possible.

WHAT IS INSANE AUTOMATISM? AN ANALYSIS OF THE CURRENT LAW

We have already established that the M'Naghten Rules set out a precise legal definition of insanity for the purposes of criminal proceedings. You may well have noted that nowhere in that definition is there reference to there being a tight correlation between medical and legal understanding. In fact, the legal and psychiatric understandings of 'insanity' can be completely different from each other in any given case. Accordingly, the fact that the accused suffers an extreme mental illness that is recognised by psychiatrists will not necessarily be sufficient to afford a defence in law. Conversely, the fact that the accused suffers from a condition that no psychiatrist would regard as 'insanity' may qualify him for the defence. So it is that we have seen such conditions as sleepwalking, epileptic seizures and certain diabetic states classified as legal insanity.

The legal definition of insanity is found in the section of the M'Naghten Rules that answers questions (ii) and (iii). By that answer, the accused is legally insane if:

> "... *at the time of committing the act, the party accused was labouring under such a defect of reason, from disease of the mind, as not to know the nature and quality of the act he was doing, or, if he did know it, that he did not know what he was doing was wrong.*"

The key elements of this definition are:

(i) The accused must be suffering from disease of the mind; and

(ii) As a result, the accused was under a defect of reason so as not to know the nature and quality of the act he was doing; or

(iii) If he did know it, that he did not know what he was doing was wrong.

In other words, once the accused is proven to be suffering from a disease of the mind, one of the two impacts that the disease has upon his state of mind must be proven. We will consider each in turn. In order to avoid any confusion, I will refer to the first impact (the nature and quality of the act) as 'limb one' of the test, and the second (knowledge that it was wrong) as 'limb two'. First, though, we should establish what is meant by 'disease of the mind'.

DISEASE OF THE MIND

It is vital to establish whether the accused was suffering from 'a defect of reason from a disease of the mind'. If the accused was unaware of the nature and quality of his act for a reason other than defect of reason due to disease of the mind, he will usually be entitled to a straightforward acquittal by virtue of the prosecution's inability to prove *mens rea*. Such a case might be where the accused claims mistake as to the nature and quality of the act. If the accused was unaware that his act was 'wrong' for some reason other than disease of the mind, he has no defence. That is because it is established law that neither ignorance of the law nor belief in the morality of one's illegal actions constitute a defence.

It is a matter of law for the judge to decide whether a defect of reason from disease of the mind has been established. The expert witnesses may testify as to the factual nature of the condition, but the ultimate decision is with the judge. That is because these are legal, rather than medical, concepts.

The phrase 'disease of the mind' does not mean that the condition must emanate from the brain, however. The caselaw indicates that any disease which sufficiently impacts the functioning of the mind is a 'disease of the mind'. In *Kemp* (1957) 1 QB 399, the defendant made an apparently motiveless and irrational attack on his wife with a hammer. He was charged with grievous bodily harm contrary to section 18 of the Offences Against the Person Act 1861. The medical evidence was to the effect that the defendant suffered from arteriosclerosis which caused a congestion of blood in his brain. As a result of that congestion, he suffered a temporary lapse of consciousness. It was during that lapse that he attacked his wife.

The defence conceded that the defendant did not know the nature and quality of his act. They further conceded that he was suffering from a defect of reason. The point of contention on appeal was whether he was suffering from a 'disease of the mind'. His representatives argued that his condition arose not from a mental disease, but a purely physical one. It was argued that it was akin to a concussion in that respect. The defence submitted that if a physical disease caused the brain cells to degenerate, then it could be categorised as a 'disease of the mind'. However, in the absence of such an effect, then this was merely a temporary interference with the working of the brain.

Devlin J, in rejecting this argument, stated at 407:

> *"The law is not concerned with the brain but with the mind, in the sense that 'mind' is ordinarily used, the mental faculties of reason, memory and understanding. If one reads for 'disease of the mind' 'disease of the brain', it would follow that in many cases pleas of insanity would not be established because it could not be proved that the brain had been affected in any way, either by degeneration of the cells or in any other way. In my judgment the condition of the brain is irrelevant and so is the question whether the condition of the mind is curable or incurable, transitory or permanent."*

It follows that so long as the condition from which the accused suffers affects his reason, memory or understanding then he will be suffering from a 'disease of the mind'. This is so even when the condition is transitory or curable.

It may be interesting to consider how this approach sits with the idea that the possibility of recurrence is a justification for imposing the label of insanity on a condition that may not warrant it medically (see Chapter One). It may be for that reason that the Court of Appeal in *Burgess* held that the possibility of recurrence is a supportive factor, but is not a conclusive one.

The courts have generally given the phrase 'disease of the mind' a broad meaning. Devlin J in *Kemp* (at 408) thought that the object of the inclusion of that phrase was to exclude *"defects of reason caused simply by brutish stupidity without rational power"*. Anything other than sheer stupidity may well be thought to qualify.

There are, however, limitations on that reach. In *Coley* (2013) EWCA Crim 223, the defendant, who had stabbed his neighbour with a hunting knife several times, was considered by medical experts to have likely suffered a psychotic episode as a result of the copious amounts of cannabis he had consumed. The Court of Appeal endorsed the trial judge's refusal to leave the defence of insanity to the jury. They held that this was a case of voluntary intoxication, and not a disease of the mind. It seems, then, that a relevant factor when deciding whether a person can legally be suffering from a 'disease of the mind' is how that 'disease' came about. We shall consider the issues in relation to intoxication further in a later chapter of this book.

DEFECT OF REASON

Once it has been established that the accused was suffering from a 'disease of the mind' at the time of the relevant act, the Court must determine whether that disease gave rise to a 'defect of reason'. In other words, the accused's powers of reasoning must be impaired. It would follow that if he possessed powers of reasoning but simply failed to use them properly, he would not fall under the scope of the M'Naghten Rules.

An illustration of that distinction in practice can be found in the case of *Clarke* (1972) 1 All ER 219. The defendant was charged with theft, having taken articles from a supermarket without paying for them. She claimed that she had not paid for them due to an absent-mindedness, resulting form depression. The trial Judge ruled that she had raised a defence of insanity, whereupon the defendant entered a guilty plea rather than face the consequences of a successful defence on that basis. Allowing the defendant's subsequent appeal against her conviction, the Court of Appeal stated (at 228):

> "... *in our judgment, the evidence fell very far short of showing either that she suffered from a defect of reason or that the consequences of that defect in reason, if any, were that she was unable to know the nature and quality of the act she was doing. The M'Naghten Rules relate to accused persons who by reason of a disease of the mind are deprived of the power of reasoning. They do not apply and never have applied to a momentary failure by someone to concentrate. The picture painted by the evidence was wholly*

consistent with the appellant being a woman who retained her ordinary powers of reason, but who was momentarily absentminded or confused and acted as she did by failing to concentrate properly on what she was doing and by failing adequately to use her mental powers."

This is an important decision to bear in mind. It may be tempting for the practitioner to presume that evidence of a 'disease of the mind' coupled with evidence of its impact on the accused's ability to reason would place the defendant within the scope of the M'Naghten Rules. The reality is not so straightforward. There is a distinction between a disease which deprives the defendant of their powers of reasoning and that which simply leads to absent-mindedness or confusion. The former falls within the ambit of the M'Naghten Rules; the latter does not.

LIMB ONE – THE NATURE AND QUALITY OF THE ACT

Having established that the accused was suffering from a disease of the mind that caused a defect of reason, we must now go on to consider whether one of the two limbs applies. By way of reminder, 'limb one' is that by virtue of the disease of the mind and defect of reason, the accused did not know the nature and quality of their act. Limb two is that, if he did know the nature and quality, he did not know that it was wrong.

A plain reading of those words indicates that 'limb one' must be considered first; limb two is only to be considered if it has been determined that the accused did know the nature and quality of the act. That has been endorsed in the Courts. In <u>Codere</u> (1916) 12 Cr App R 21, the defendant murdered his wife by cutting her throat. He argued that he had thought he was cutting a loaf of bread. On appeal, the Court stated that the approach to the M'Naghten test was to, first, consider whether the defendant knew the nature and quality of his act.

If he did, then the court must go on to consider whether the defendant knew that the act was wrong.

In that case, the Court made clear that 'nature and quality of the act' refers to the physical nature and quality of the act – not whether it was morally or legally wrong. That aspect fell to be considered in the second limb of the test.

For example, where a person's acts are involuntary due to his being in an unconscious state, he cannot be said to know the nature and quality of his act (*Sullivan* (1983) 2 All ER 673). Quite simply, he does not know what he is doing.

LIMB TWO – KNOWLEDGE THAT THE ACT IS WRONG

Legal Wrong or Moral Wrong?

Having established that the defendant was physically aware of what he was doing, the second limb requires the court to consider whether he knew that the act was wrong. The question follows, then, what is meant by 'wrong'? Is this a moral imputation, or a legal one?

The answer seems to be as follows. First, if the defendant thought that his actions were wrong according to the ordinary standard adopted by reasonable men, he is taken to know that the action is wrong. Secondly, if he knew that his actions were illegal then he is taken to have known that the act was wrong. In *Codere*, Lord Reading stated as follows:

> "*If the accused does know either that his act is morally wrong according to the ordinary standard adopted by reasonable men or that it is legally wrong then it cannot be said that he does not know he was doing what was wrong.*"

The former does not raise much issue. It is a well-accepted principle of the criminal justice system that ignorance of the law is not a defence.

It does not seem too controversial to expand that to interpretation of the M'Naghten test.

However, the latter has raised some controversy. If a person knows that what they have done is illegal, then it seems that it matters not whether he genuinely thought that it was right according to the standard adopted by reasonable men. In *Windle* (1952) 2 QB 826, the defendant had killed his wife. He was a man described as being of 'weak character', in an unhappy marriage to a woman 18 years his senior. Evidence was given that his wife was herself suffering from mental health problems and was always talking about committing suicide. The defendant became obsessed with her ideations and discussed it with his workmates until they were reportedly tired of hearing about it. Eventually, one of them flippantly said to him "give her a dozen aspirins". Accordingly, shortly afterwards, the defendant gave his wife 100 aspirin tablets. She died as a result. When apprehended by police, the defendant remarked to them that he 'supposed he would be hanged for it'.

At trial, the defendant entered a not guilty plea by virtue of insanity. The defence expert said that the defendant suffered from a communicated insanity, known as *folie a deux*, arising when a person is in constant attendance on a person of unsound mind. The defendant was convicted.

The Court of Appeal considered what was meant by the term 'wrong' in the M'Naghten Rules. It had been common ground that the defendant had remarked to the police that he expected to be hanged for what he had done. This demonstrated an understanding that the act was unlawful. In holding that a knowledge that the act was unlawful was sufficient to demonstrate that the defendant knew it was 'wrong', the Court of Appeal stated at 833 (*per* Goddard CJ):

> "*Courts of law can only distinguish between that which is in accordance with law and that which is contrary to law. There are*

> *many acts which, to use an expression which is to be found in some of the old cases, are contrary to the law of God and man. For instance, in the Decalogue will be found the laws "Thou shalt not kill" and "Thou shalt not steal." Those acts are contrary to the law of man and also to the law of God. If the seventh commandment is taken, "Thou shalt not commit adultery," although that is contrary to the law of God, so far as the criminal law is concerned it is not contrary to the law of man. That does not mean that the law encourages adultery; I only say that it is not a criminal offence. The law cannot embark on the question, and it would be an unfortunate thing if it were left to juries to consider whether some particular act was morally right or wrong. The test must be whether it is contrary to law."*

We can see that this reasoning is sound in the majority of situations. After all, consider the case of a pious man who murders his adulterous spouse. The law cannot exempt him from punishment because he believes that she has wronged him, and he is morally entitled to take her life. Consider further the cases where a person has wreaked horrific acts on sex workers, under some warped notion that their lives are worth less than those of others. In such cases, the law cannot make allowance for the moral beliefs of an individual when it violently affronts the interests of society.

What, though, of the case where a person's defect of reason leads them to genuinely that what they are doing is right, even if they know that the law is against them? For example, a person such as Wilde who seems to have been operating under a delusion that he was doing what was ultimately best for his wife. It seems uncomfortable to punish a person for an act which they genuinely thought was 'right' in the moral sense of the word, not because they have ignored reason or labour under bigoted ideas, but because their mental faculties are so damaged that they did not have the ordinary faculties of reason.

The issue was more recently considered in *Johnson* (2007) EWCA Crim 1978. In that case, the appellant had been convicted of one count of causing grievous bodily harm with intent, contrary to section 18 of the Offences Against the Person Act 1861. At the time of the incident in question, the appellant had been suffering from auditory and visual hallucinations. He believed that those around him were surrounded by 'firewalls' and had been, in his words, 'noncing' his sister. In that state of mind, he burst into his neighbour's flat one day and violently stabbed him, all the while shouting incomprehensibly.

Examining psychiatrists were of the view that the appellant knew the nature and quality of his act and knew that what he was doing was illegal. However, in his delusional state, he absolutely believed that he was morally right.

The Court of Appeal considered the meaning of 'wrong' within the M'Naghten Rules. The Court affirmed the principle set out in *Windle* that if the accused knew that what they did was legally wrong, they knew it was 'wrong' within the meaning of the Rules. At paragraphs 21 to 24:

> "*[acknowledging 'persuasive' arguments of the Australian Court as to the] difficulties and internal inconsistencies which can arise from the application of the M'Naghten Rules, particularly if the decision in Windle is correct. But we return to the case of Windle in order to indicate the clear terms in which the court there construed the proper application of the answer to the second and third question to which we have referred. The Lord Chief Justice at the end of his judgment in that case stated in clear terms the following:*
>
>> "*In the opinion of the court, there is no doubt that the word 'wrong' in the M'Naghten Rules means contrary to law and does not have some vague meaning which may vary according to the opinion of different persons whether a particular act might or might not be justified.*"

22. This statement of the law is unequivocal and has been, so far as we are aware, been doubted since then in this court.

23. The fact, however, remains that, although that has been the basis upon which the textbooks have set out the rule and its proper meaning, there is some evidence which is contained in material in articles, in particular, by Professor MacKay, for example, "Yet more facts about the Insanity Defence" [1999] Crim LR 714, that courts may have on occasions been prepared to approach the issue on a more relaxed basis. Nonetheless, in our view, the strict position at the moment remains as stated in Windle and in the passages in Archbold, Blackstone and Smith and Hogan to which we have referred.

24. This area, however, is a notorious area for debate and quite rightly so. There is room for reconsideration of rules and, in particular, rules which have their genesis in the early years of the 19th century. But it does not seem to us that that debate is a debate which can properly take place before us at this level in this case. For those reasons we dismiss the appeal."

As alluded to in the Court's judgment, commentators have indicated that this strict approach is both unsatisfactory and is not followed in practice. The 1999 article quoted by the Court, and a further 2006 article by the same authors (*Yet More Facts About the Insanity Plea* (2006) Crim LR 399) indicate that the trial courts make little distinction between the awareness of legal and moral wrongs. In 1975, the Butler Committee in its report *Report of the Committee on Mentally Abnormal Offenders* (1975) Cmnd 6244, commented that knowledge of the law was not an appropriate test for ascribing responsibility to those who are mentally disordered. The Committee considered it to be a narrow ground of exemption, given that persons who are extremely disturbed generally know that crimes such as murder and arson are illegal.

It is also interesting to note that the High Court of Australia has considered and rejected the *Windle* interpretation. In the Australian case of *Stapleton* (1953) 86 CLR 358, the Court analysed in detail the English law before and after M'Naghten. The Court's view was that if the defendant believed his actions to be right according to the ordinary standard of reasonable people, then he was entitled to be acquitted – notwithstanding that he knew it to be legally wrong.

Whatever the reservations of the English courts, however, the law remains clear: if the accused knows that his actions are unlawful, then he knows that his act is 'wrong'. His moral view is irrelevant.

The Role of Delusions

What if the accused was operating under a delusion as to fact, so that the factual matrix in which he was acting was different from that in which everyone else was operating?

This question was in fact asked, and answered, in answer (iv) of the M'Naghten Rules:

> "*The fourth question which your Lordships have proposed to us is this: 'If a person under an insane delusion as to existing facts, commits an offence in consequence thereof, is he thereby excused?' To which question the answer must of course depend on the nature of the delusion: but, making the same assumption as we did before, namely, that he labours under such partial delusion only, and is not in other respects insane, we think he must be considered in the same situation as to responsibility as if the facts with respect to which the delusion exists were real. For example, if under the influence of his delusion he supposes another man to be in the act of attempting to take away his life, and he kills that man, as he supposes, in self-defence, he would be exempt from punishment. If his delusion was that the deceased had inflicted a serious injury to his character and*

fortune, and he killed him in revenge for such supposed injury, he would be liable to punishment."

The Judges at that time considered that the person's delusions (if accepted) were to be considered as if they were the actual factual situation. Therefore, if the person's actions would have been excusable in the matrix as he believed it to be, they would be excusable before the court.

Modern judgments have resiled somewhat from this viewpoint. In <u>Oye</u> (2013) EWCA Crim 1725, the appellant had been convicted of causing grievous bodily harm and affray. He had been discovered behaving in an odd manner in a café. When police arrived, he was hiding in a pocket in the ceiling, giving nonsensical sounding reasons for being there and throwing crockery at the officers. They managed to get hold of him and take him into custody. When in custody, the appellant tried to escape. In the process, he knocked one officer to the ground and fractured another officer's jaw. When more officers got to the cell, he was thrashing violently.

At trial, the appellant's account was that he was in a delusional state, whereupon he believed that the police officers were attacking him and he had to lash out in self-defence. Expert witnesses testified to the effect that he was in the grips of a psychotic episode at the time. The jury not only rejected the assertion that he was acting in self-defence, but rejected the defence of insanity.

The question on appeal was whether a defendant was entitled to an acquittal on the grounds of self-defence, where he mistakenly but honestly believed that he was being attacked due to his delusions. The Court of Appeal rejected that idea, stating at paragraph 47:

"The position remains, as we think plain from the provisions of s.76 of the 2008 Act, that the second limb of self-defence does include an objective element by reference to reasonableness, even if there may

also be a subjective element: see in particular s.76(6) and see also the decision in R v Keane & McGrath [2011] EWCA Crim 2514 . An insane person cannot set the standards of reasonableness as to the degree of force used by reference to his own insanity. In truth it makes as little sense to talk of the reasonable lunatic as it did, in the context of cases on provocation, to talk of the reasonable glue-sniffer."

In other words, the standards of the 'reasonable man' inherent in the self-defence test are standards of a sane reasonable man. In that particular case, in any event, the Court of Appeal could not find that the jury's decision to reject the insanity defence could be justified, given that the expert evidence was unchallenged. They therefore allowed the appeal on that basis only and imposed an absolute discharge.

CHAPTER THREE

NON-INSANE AUTOMATISM

In general terms, we know that automatism means the performance of actions without conscious thought or intention. We have discussed in some detail what is meant by insane automatism – i.e. where the lack of conscious thought or intention is due to a disease of the mind. However, that leaves space in the criminal law where a person commits an act involuntarily but this cannot be attributed to a disease of the mind. This space is occupied by the law of non-insane automatism (also termed 'sane automatism' by some authors).

WHAT DOES NON-INSANE AUTOMATISM MEAN?

There is no clear definition of non-insane automatism. We saw in Chapter One that the courts have drawn a distinction between 'internal' and 'external' causes. The former broadly means that insane automatism applies; the latter means that non-insane automatism applies.

Such a distinction is relatively straightforward when we consider the extreme examples. For example, nobody could dispute that insanity applies when the accused is in a severe mentally ill state that renders him incapable of knowing what he is doing. Equally, there could be little dispute that a person cannot and should not be subject to the law of insane automatism when their loss of control was due to, for example, a swarm of bees flying through their car window, causing them to crash the car that they have been driving. The swarm constitutes an indisputably external factor.

However, as we shall see when we analyse the 'special cases' in later chapters, the internal/external distinction is less helpful when it comes to cases that fall somewhere in the middle of those two extremes.

What, for example, of the case where a person suffers a heart attack whilst driving, which causes him to crash the car into another? He cannot be said to have been afflicted by an external cause. However, he is not suffering from a disease of the mind. As we shall see, the law in relation to insane and non-insane automatism has attempted to produce answers to these questions, though the results may not always be said to be satisfactory.

GUIDANCE FROM THE COURTS ON THE MEANING OF NON-INSANE AUTOMATISM

The courts have given some further assistance as to what exactly is meant by non-insane automatism.

Bratty v Attorney-General for Northern Ireland (1963) AC 386 was one such case. We will consider the facts of that case in more detail when we come to analyse epilepsy and the law of automatism. In brief, the accused in that case had strangled a girl in his car with her own stocking. At trial, the evidence was that he might have been suffering from psychomotor epilepsy which could cause ignorance of the nature and quality of the acts done. At trial, perhaps unusually, both the defences of insane and non-insane automatism were raised. The trial judge left the defence of insanity only to the jury, which was duly rejected.

The accused was convicted and appealed to the Court of Appeal of Northern Ireland. Following their dismissal of the appeal, the case made its way to the House of Lords. Their Lordships then undertook an analysis of the differences between insane and non-insane automatism.

In the course of those discussions, Kilmuir LC, at 401, cited without disapproval the analysis of the Court of Appeal in that case that automatism is a concept:

"*...connoting the state of a person who, though capable of action, is not conscious of what he is doing. In this connection the word does not mean the doing of what is involuntary in the sense that the doer, while knowing what he is doing, cannot resist the impulse to do it. It means unconscious involuntary action, and it is a defence because the mind does not go with what is being done.*"

At 409 to 410, Lord Denning gave the following opinion; it provides a detailed analysis of the circumstances in which non-insane automatism might be an appropriate defence:

"*No act is punishable if it is done involuntarily: and an involuntary act in this context – some people nowadays prefer to speak of it as "automatism" – means an act which is done by the muscles without any control by the mind, such as a spasm, a reflex action or a convulsion; or an act done by a person who is not conscious of what he is doing, such as an act done whilst suffering from concussion or whilst sleep-walking. The point was well put by Stephen J. in 1889: "Can anyone doubt that a man who, though he might be perfectly sane, committed what would otherwise be a crime in a state of somnambulism, would be entitled to be acquitted? and why is this? Simply because he would not know what he was doing,"* […] *The term "involuntary act" is, however, capable of wider connotations: and to prevent confusion it is to be observed that in the criminal law an act is not to be regarded as an involuntary act simply because the doer does not remember it. When a man is charged with dangerous driving, it is no defence to him to say "I don't know what happened. I cannot remember a thing,"* […] *Loss of memory afterwards is never a defence in itself, so long as he was conscious at the time*

[…]

Nor is an act to be regarded as an involuntary act simply because the doer could not control his impulse to do it. When a man is charged with murder, and it appears that he knew what he was doing, but he could not resist it, then his assertion "I couldn't help myself" is no defence in itself, see Attorney-General for South Australia v. Brown 65 : though it may go towards a defence of diminished responsibility, in places where that defence is available [...] but it does not render his act involuntary so as to entitle him to an unqualified acquittal. Nor is an act to be regarded as an involuntary act simply because it is unintentional or its consequences are unforeseen. When a man is charged with dangerous driving, it is no defence for him to say, however truly, "I did not mean to drive dangerously." There is said to be an absolute prohibition against that offence, whether he had a guilty mind or not, see Hill v. Baxter 67 by Lord Goddard C.J. But even though it is absolutely prohibited, nevertheless he has a defence if he can show that it was an involuntary act in the sense that he was unconscious at the time and did not know what he was doing

[...]

Another thing to be observed is that it is not every involuntary act which leads to a complete acquittal. Take first an involuntary act which proceeds from a state of drunkenness. If the drunken man is so drunk that he does not know what he is doing, he has a defence to any charge, such as murder or wounding with intent, in which a specific intent is essential, but he is still liable to be convicted of manslaughter or unlawful wounding for which no specific intent is necessary

[...]

Again, if the involuntary act proceeds from a disease of the mind, it gives rise to a defence of insanity, but not to a defence of automatism. Suppose a crime is committed by a man in a state of automatism or clouded consciousness due to a recurrent disease of the mind. Such an act is no doubt involuntary, but it does not give rise to an unqualified acquittal, for that would mean that he would be let at large to do it again. The only proper verdict is one which ensures that the person who suffers from the disease is kept secure in a hospital so as not to be a danger to himself or others. That is, a verdict of guilty but insane.

Once you exclude all the cases I have mentioned, it is apparent that the category of involuntary acts is very limited. So limited, indeed, that until recently there was hardly any reference in the English books to this so-called defence of automatism."

The key points to note from these observations of Lord Denning are as follows:

(i) A person is not to be found guilty for an act they have committed involuntarily;

(ii) An involuntary act by a person means either one where the person is aware of what is happening but cannot control it, such as a muscle spasm, or where they are not conscious of what they are doing – such as when they are unconscious;

(iii) In the criminal law, an act is not involuntary simply because the person cannot remember doing it;

(iv) In the criminal law, an act is not involuntary simply because the person could not resist the impulse to do it;

(v) In the criminal law, an act is not involuntary because its consequences are unintentional or unforeseen;

(vi) Involuntary acts that are precipitated by voluntary intoxication will not lead to an acquittal, unless the crime is one of specific intent (we will discuss this in the specific chapter on intoxication later in this book);

(vii) If the involuntary act is caused by a disease of the mind then it gives rise to a defence of insanity, so as to allow the court discretion to direct the accused to receive medical help.

The Court of Appeal in the more recent case of *Coley* (2013) EWCA Crim 223 confirms that involuntary action means that the accused must have suffered a complete destruction of voluntary control. A partial loss of control will not suffice. That does not mean, though, that the accused needs to be unconscious:

> "*[22] .. Automatism, if it occurs, results in a complete acquittal on the grounds that the act was not that of the defendant at all. It has been variously described. The essence of it is that the movements or actions of the defendant at the material time were wholly involuntary. The better expression is complete destruction of voluntary control: Watmore v Jenkins [1962] 2 QB 572 and Attorney-General's Reference (No 2 of 1992) [1994] QB 91 . Examples which have been given in the past include the driver attacked by a swarm of bees or the man under hypnosis. 'Involuntary' is not the same as 'irrational'; indeed it needs sharply to be distinguished from it.*
>
> **23.** *In the present case the doctors were asked several times whether the defendant was acting "consciously" when he did what he did. We understand the difficulties of selecting appropriate adverbs, but this one carries some risk of difficulty. He was plainly not unconscious, in the sense of comatose. But automatism does not require that, and if it did it would be even more exceptional than it undoubtedly is.*"

GUIDANCE FROM THE LAW COMMISSION ON THE MEANING OF NON-INSANE AUTOMATISM

In 2013 the Law Commission published a discussion paper entitled *Criminal Liability: Insanity and Automatism*. Although merely a discussion paper, it provides some interesting considerations for what might be done with those cases that do not neatly fit into the 'internal/external' distinction. At paragraphs 5.13 to 5.17, the Commission suggests the following three categories of non-insane automatism.

Category One: Automatism from Internal Malfunctioning but Not a Disease of the Mind

An example of such a category is given: where an accused, who is driving, experiences a cramp in his leg. As a result, his foot slams down on the accelerator and he crashes the car. This scenario is akin to my example of the man who has a heart attack whilst driving. In both, there is no external factor to trigger the symptom. The cause is purely internal. Yet there has been no impairment of the accused's mental faculties, and no disease of the mind. The Law Commission notes that such a case has never been directly considered by the courts.

It suggests that such a situation should lead to an acquittal on the grounds of non-insane automatism. At paragraph 5.15 of the discussion paper, the Commission recognises the departure from the orthodox internal/external distinction, but submits that this must be the best way to reflect a case where a person loses control due to an internal factor that is not a disease of the mind.

Category Two: Automatism as a Result of Ingestion of a Substance

The Law Commission suggests that automatism caused by ingestion of a substance results in a complete acquittal on the grounds of non-insane automatism, unless the accused was at fault in either inducing or failing to avoid the loss of control. So the patient who takes a prescribed drug not commonly known to cause involuntary aggression is to be acquitted if the drug in fact has that effect. Conversely, the person who voluntarily imbibes alcohol, knowing that it can make him quick tempered and irrational, has no defence in law.

Category Three: Automatism Arising From an External Factor Other than Ingestion of a Substance

Examples given by the Law Commission in relation to this category are where the accused has been stung by a wasp while driving, or struck by a stone thrown up from the road and acted reflexively. Such a situation will result in a complete acquittal.

CHAPTER FOUR

DIMINISHED RESPONSIBILITY – A THIRD OPTION

Both insane and non-insane automatism are capable of applying to any offence. In cases of murder, however, there is a third defence relevant to an accused's ability to control themselves at the time of the act: 'diminished responsibility'.

The defence does not apply to any offences other than murder. It is not even a defence to attempted murder. Equally, it cannot be raised on a finding of unfitness to plead.

It is a partial defence – meaning that if it is successfully argued, it results in a finding that the defendant is guilty of manslaughter. It holds a reverse burden of proof – in other words, the onus is on the defendant to prove the elements of the defence.

BACKGROUND TO DIMINISHED RESPONSIBILITY

Section 2 of the Homicide Act 1957 ("the 1957 Act") introduced the statutory defence of 'diminished responsibility' for the first time. Under that provision, the defence was available on a charge of murder where the defendant could prove that he was:

(i) Suffering from an abnormality of mind;

(ii) Arising from a condition of arrested or retarded development of mind, from any inherent causes or induced by disease or injury;

(iii) Which substantially impaired his mental responsibility.

Following a number of calls for reform over the next sixty years, section 2 of the 1957 Act was reformed in 2009.

THE CURRENT LEGISLATION

Section 52 of the Coroners and Justice Act 2009 reformed section 2 of the 1957 Act, and was enacted in October 2010. As a consequence, section 2 now states:

> *"2.— Persons suffering from diminished responsibility.*
>
> *(1) A person ("D") who kills or is a party to the killing of another is not to be convicted of murder if D was suffering from an abnormality of mental functioning which—*
>
> *(a) arose from a recognised medical condition,*
>
> *(b) substantially impaired D's ability to do one or more of the things mentioned in subsection (1A), and*
>
> *(c) provides an explanation for D's acts and omissions in doing or being a party to the killing.*
>
> *(1A) Those things are—*
>
> *(a) to understand the nature of D's conduct;*
>
> *(b) to form a rational judgment;*
>
> *(c) to exercise self-control.*
>
> *(1B) For the purposes of subsection (1)(c), an abnormality of mental functioning provides an explanation for D's conduct if it causes, or is a significant contributory factor in causing, D to carry out that conduct.*

(2) On a charge of murder, it shall be for the defence to prove that the person charged is by virtue of this section not liable to be convicted of murder.

(3) A person who but for this section would be liable, whether as principal or as accessory, to be convicted of murder shall be liable instead to be convicted of manslaughter.

(4) The fact that one party to a killing is by virtue of this section not liable to be convicted of murder shall not affect the question whether the killing amounted to murder in the case of any other party to it."

THE ELEMENTS OF THE OFFENCE

The elements of the offence are as follows:

(i) The defendant was suffering from an abnormality of mental functioning;

(ii) The abnormality arises from a recognised medical condition;

(iii) The defendant's mental ability is substantially impaired as a consequence;

(iv) The abnormality of mental functioning must be a cause or contributory cause of the defendant's relevant actions.

ELEMENT ONE: ABNORMALITY OF MENTAL FUNCTIONING

You may have noted that the old law referred to 'abnormality of mind', whereas the current law refers to 'abnormality of mental functioning'. Our analysis of the cases in relation to insane automatism indicates that the courts have interpreted the word 'mind' to include faculties of mental reasoning and functioning.

The term 'mind' under the old law was held by the Court in *Byrne* (1960) 2 QB 396 at 403 to "*mean a state of mind so different from that of ordinary human being that the reasonable man would term it abnormal*".

The current phrasing seems to import something more of a medical interpretation than that being considered in *Byrne*. So it is that the current cases tend to involve expert opinion as a matter of course when this defence is raised.

ELEMENT TWO: RECOGNISED MEDICAL CONDITION

In the original iteration of the statute, Parliament proscribed a list of recognised causes for the relevant abnormality of mind. The current iteration widens the ambit by simply stating that the abnormality should be caused by a 'recognised medical condition'.

At the same time, the explicit reference to a 'medical condition' will all but necessitate a medical diagnosis. Of course, there is no further curtailment on the type of medical condition; it would follow that any physical or psychiatric condition causing an abnormality of mental functioning would suffice.

Note that whilst being drunk is not a recognised medical condition, alcoholic dependency is; it would seem that the latter, then, would qualify under the current statutory provision.

The fact that the medical condition must be one that is 'recognised' should not be overlooked. This requirement exists to prevent spurious, idiosyncratic diagnoses being advanced as reliable bases for the defence. In *Dowds* (2012) EWCA Crim 281, the Court of Appeal held that it was necessary for the condition to be included in one of the diagnostic manuals – although it might not always be sufficient for it to be so included. The Court observed that the diagnostic manuals are extremely broad and include a number of conditions of questionable legal value – examples given were pyromania, unhappiness, suspiciousness and marked evasiveness.

ELEMENT THREE: A SUBSTANTIAL IMPAIRMENT OF MENTAL ABILITY

The old legislation was concerned with the accused's mental responsibility. The current legislation has changed the focus to the accused's mental ability.

The meaning of the term 'substantially' under the current legislation was considered in <u>Ramchurn</u> (2010) EWCA Crim 194. In that case, Lord Judge CJ, remarking that 'substantially' is an ordinary English word, said at paragraph 13:

> " *'Substantially' is an ordinary English word which appears in the context of a statutory provision creating a special defence which, to reflect reduced mental responsibility for what otherwise would be murderous actions, reduces the crime from murder to manslaughter. Its presence in the statute is deliberate. It is designed to ensure that the murderous activity of a defendant should not result in a conviction for manslaughter rather than murder on account of any impairment of mental responsibility, however trivial and insignificant; but equally that the defence should be available without the defendant having to show that his mental responsibility for his actions was so grossly impaired as to be extinguished. That is the purpose of this defence and this language.*"

More recently, the Supreme Court considered the interpretation of section 2 of the 1957 Act in the case of <u>Golds</u> (2016) UKSC 61. The certified questions were a) whether the judge is required to direct the jury on the meaning of 'substantial'; and b) whether it is to be defined as 'something more than merely trivial' or alternatively in a way that connotes more than this.

In considering the decision, the Supreme Court held at paragraphs 27 et sequitur:

> *27. The admirably concise submissions of Mr Etherington QC for the appellant correctly point out that as a matter simply of dictionary definition, "substantial" is capable of meaning either (1) "present rather than illusory or fanciful, thus having some substance" or (2) "important or weighty", as in "a substantial meal" or "a substantial salary". The first meaning could fairly be paraphrased as "having any effect more than the merely trivial", whereas the second meaning cannot.*
>
> *[…]*
>
> *28. The foregoing review of the authorities clearly shows that in the context of diminished responsibility the expression "substantially" has always been held, when the issue has been confronted, to be used in the second of the senses identified above.*
>
> *[…]*
>
> *30. There is no basis for thinking that when the same expression was carried forward into the new formulation of diminished responsibility any change of sense was intended. The adverb "substantially" is applied now, as before, to the verb "impaired". In the absence of any indication to the contrary, Parliament is to be taken to have adopted the established sense in which this word has been used for 50 years.*
>
> *[…]*
>
> *36. This use of the expression accords with principle. Diminished responsibility effects a radical alteration in the offence of which a defendant is convicted. The context is a homicide. By definition, before any question of diminished responsibility can arise, the homicide must have been done with murderous intent, to kill or to*

do grievous bodily harm, and without either provocation or self-defence. Whilst it is true that at one end of the scale of responsibility the sentence in a case of diminished responsibility may be severe, or indeed an indefinite life sentence owing to the risk which the defendant presents to the public, the difference between a conviction for murder and a conviction for manslaughter is of considerable importance both for the public and for those connected with the deceased. It is just that where a substantial impairment is demonstrated, the defendant is convicted of the lesser offence and not of murder. But it is appropriate, as it always has been, for the reduction to the lesser offence to be occasioned where there is a weighty reason for it and not merely a reason which just passes the trivial."

This interpretation of the Supreme Court appears, then, to narrow the meaning accorded to the word by the Court of Appeal in *Ramchurn*. The Court of Appeal's reading of it placed the term within the wide range between something more than 'any impairment' and something less than 'total extinguishing of mental responsibility'. The Supreme Court's decision elevates the meaning of 'substantial' to mean something more akin to 'significant'.

ELEMENT FOUR: PROVIDES AN EXPLANATION FOR THE KILLING

Section 521(c) indicates that the abnormality of mental functioning must provide an explanation for the killing. It is further expanded by section 52(1B) which states:

"For the purposes of subsection (1)(c), an abnormality of mental functioning provides an explanation for D's conduct if it causes, or is a significant contributory factor in causing, D to carry out that conduct."

It is important to note that the abnormality of mental functioning need not be the only cause of the conduct. It need not even be the primary cause, so long as it is a 'significant contributory factor'. Does this mean that there needs to be 'but for' style causation, or merely that it was a significant element present?

The parliamentary debates around the enactment of the defence provides some assistance. In debates, the ministers stated that the partial defence should not succeed where random coincidence brought together the person's conduct and their medical condition. There must be something more than a merely trivial factor, albeit there was no requirement that the defence should prove that it was the only cause, main cause or even the most important factor (see Hansard, HC, 4 March 2009, col 416).

This means that where the accused is acted due to jealousy, anger or some other emotion, they may avail themselves of the defence where their mental disorder was also a significant contributor, even if their primary reason was something the law does not consider an excuse.

CHAPTER FIVE

SPECIAL CASES – EPILEPSY

In earlier chapters, I have alluded to the fact that the treatment of epilepsy by the criminal law appears to run contrary to common or medical sense. It is true that claims of automatism based on epilepsy are not often before the courts. A 2007 study by Mackay and Reuber found that in the period 1975 to 2001, epilepsy only accounted for 13 special verdicts (*Epilepsy and the Defence of Insanity – Time For Change?* Mackay and Reuber, 2007 CLR 782). However, when they have appeared before the courts, the courts have consistently classed it as a form of insane automatism.

On 22 December 1960, a 26-year-old man named George Bratty suddenly and violently strangled 18-year-old Josephine Fitzsimmons in his car. Her abandoned body was found later that night. When Mr Bratty was interviewed by police, he admitted strangling the girl with her own stocking, but claimed that a 'blackness' had come over him that he could not explain.

Medical evidence was subsequently obtained which indicated that Mr Bratty was suffering from psychomotor epilepsy at the time, which may have prevented him from knowing what he was doing.

At trial, the defence raised three defences. The first, which was the primary defence and was submitted to be the 'proper' one, was that he was not guilty on the basis of non-insane automatism. The second was that Mr Bratty was incapable of forming the requisite intent due to impairment of his mental condition and so the verdict should be manslaughter. The third was that, if the jury rejected both other possibilities, Mr Bratty was suffering from insane automatism at the time. The trial judge refused to leave the first two defences to the jury.

It was that refusal which was the subject of appeal to the Court of Appeal and then to the House of Lords.

In rejecting the appeal, Lord Denning remarked at 412:

> "*Upon the other point discussed by Devlin J., namely, what is a "disease of the mind" within the M'Naughten Rules, I would agree with him that this is a question for the judge. The major mental diseases, which the doctors call psychoses, such as schizophrenia, are clearly diseases of the mind. But in Charlson's case, Barry J. seems to have assumed that other diseases such as epilepsy or cerebral tumour are not diseases of the mind, even when they are such as to manifest themselves in violence. I do not agree with this. It seems to me that any mental disorder which has manifested itself in violence and is prone to recur is a disease of the mind. At any rate it is the sort of disease for which a person should be detained in hospital rather than be given an unqualified acquittal.*"

It may seem an affront to medical or common sense to label epilepsy as a form of insanity. However, the issue may be the use of the label 'insanity' and the stigma attached thereto, rather than the decision to apply the M'Naghten Rules to epileptic seizures. Where it is clear that there is a risk of recurrence but, by virtue of the act being involuntary, detention within the prison system will not address such a risk, then hospital detention is the only option left. It cannot be conscionable to allow a person who has involuntarily killed before to be released with nothing more than a hope and a prayer that he does not do so again. The only reasonable conclusion under the current law, then, is to place epilepsy under the insane automatism regime.

Some twenty years later, the House of Lords was again faced with a case involving the inter-relation between epileptic seizures and the criminal law in the case of <u>Sullivan</u> (1983) 2 All ER 673.

Mr Sullivan suffered from epilepsy which was controlled by medication. However, one day when he was visiting his 86-year-old neighbour, he was subject to a violent seizure. In the throes of this seizure, he kicked a fellow visitor who was around 80 years of age. Mr Sullivan kicked this elderly man around the head and body. He was charged with offences of causing grievous bodily harm.

Mr Sullivan's case was that he had no recollection of the incident. There was evidence produced to the effect that he likely committed the act whilst in the third stage of his seizure, during which his body would move but Mr Sullivan would not be aware or conscious of those movements. The trial judge held that the defence raised was one of insanity. Mr Sullivan consequently changed his plea to guilty and appealed the trial judge's ruling.

In the House of Lords, Lord Diplock – with sympathy for Mr Sullivan – concluded that the trial judge had been correct to classify Mr Sullivan's epileptic seizure as a form of legal insanity. In reaching this conclusion, he said, at 173:

> *"My Lords, it is natural to feel reluctant to attach the label of insanity to a sufferer from psychomotor epilepsy of the kind to which Mr. Sullivan was subject, even though the expression in the context of a special verdict of "not guilty by reason of insanity" is a technical one which includes a purely temporary and intermittent suspension of the mental faculties of reason, memory and understanding resulting from the occurrence of an epileptic fit. But the label is contained in the current statute, it has appeared in this statute's predecessors ever since 1800. It does not lie within the power of the courts to alter it. Only Parliament can do that. It has done so twice; it could do so once again.*
>
> *Sympathise though I do with Mr. Sullivan, I see no other course open to your Lordships than to dismiss this appeal."*

It is worth noting that in *Sullivan*, unlike in *Bratty*, the medical experts were of the firm view that the short duration of the seizure (i.e. less than a day) meant that it could not be a disease of the mind. In rejecting the submission that medical opinion should dictate the legal conclusion, Lord Diplock opined at 172:

> "*The nomenclature adopted by the medical profession may change from time to time; Bratty was tried in 1961. But the meaning of the expression "disease of the mind" as the cause of "a defect of reason" remains unchanged for the purposes of the application of the M'Naghten Rules. I agree with what was said by Devlin J. in Reg. v. Kemp [1957] 1 Q.B. 399, 407, that "mind" in the M'Naghten Rules is used in the ordinary sense of the mental faculties of reason, memory and understanding. If the effect of a disease is to impair these faculties so severely as to have either of the consequences referred to in the latter part of the rules, it matters not whether the aetiology, of the impairment is organic, as in epilepsy, or functional, or whether the impairment itself is permanent or is transient and intermittent, provided that it subsisted at the time of commission of the act. The purpose of the legislation relating to the defence of insanity, ever since its origin in 1800, has been to protect society against recurrence of the dangerous conduct. The duration of a temporary suspension of the mental faculties of reason, memory and understanding, particularly if, as in Mr. Sullivan's case, it is recurrent, cannot on any rational ground be relevant to the application by the courts of the M'Naghten Rules, though it may be relevant to the course adopted by the Secretary of State, to whom the responsibility for how the defendant is to be dealt with passes after the return of the special verdict of "not guilty by reason of insanity."*

In this passage, then, Lord Diplock places emphasis on the need to identify and assuage the possibility of recurrence of the activity in question. In that respect, the court's approach may well differ significantly from that of medical experts, who will apply a scientific process of categorisation based on the features of the illness itself.

CHAPTER SIX

SPECIAL CASES – DIABETES

The treatment of diabetes perhaps best illustrates the problem with relying upon the 'internal' / 'external' distinction to decide between insane and non-insane automatism. Consider the following two cases.

The first is *Quick and Paddison* (1973) QB 910. Quick and Paddison were nurses employed at a hospital. They were convicted of assault occasioning actual bodily harm to a paraplegic patient.

Mr Quick sought to establish a defence of non-insane automatism. He presented medical evidence to show that he was diabetic, and at the time of the assault had eaten insufficient food to neutralise the insulin he had taken. He was suffering from hypoglycaemia as a result. The trial judge ruled that Quick had raised a defence of insanity. Consequently, Quick changed his plea to guilty and appealed on the ground that the judge's ruling was wrong.

Allowing the appeal, Lawson LJ delivered the reasoning of the court at 922 and 923:

> "*In this case Quick's alleged mental condition, if it ever existed, was not caused by his diabetes but by his use of the insulin prescribed by his doctor. Such malfunctioning of his mind as there was, was caused by an external factor and not by a bodily disorder in the nature of a disease which disturbed the working of his mind. It follows in our judgment that Quick was entitled to have his defence of automatism left to the jury and that Bridge J.'s ruling as to the effect of the medical evidence called by him was wrong.*"

In Quick's case, therefore, the Court held that insulin was the external factor causing the involuntary act, and so his condition could legally be defined as non-insane automatism.

The second case is *Hennessy* (1989) 2 All ER 9. Mr Hennessy was charged with taking a conveyance and driving whilst disqualified. He was a diabetic. In defence, he claimed that at the time he was suffering from stress, anxiety and depression. As a consequence, he had failed to take his proper dose of insulin and was suffering from hyperglycaemia when he committed the relevant acts. He sought to advance the legal defence of non-insane automatism. The trial judge ruled that he had advanced only a defence of insane automatism. Hennessy pleaded guilty and then appealed on the basis that the trial judge's ruling was wrong.

Dismissing the appeal, the Court distinguished Hennessy's situation from that of Quick. At 293:

> "…*in Quick's case the fact that his condition was, or may have been due to the injections of insulin, meant that the malfunction was due to an external factor and not to the disease. The drug it was that caused the hypoglycaemia, the low blood sugar. As suggested in another passage of the judgment of Lawton L.J. (at p. 922G–H), hyperglycaemia, high blood sugar, caused by an inherent defect, and not corrected by insulin is a disease, and if, as the defendant was asserting here, it does cause a malfunction of the mind, then the case may fall within M'Naghten Rules."*

The Court further rejected appellant counsel's submission that Mr Hennessy's stress, anxiety and depression were external factors that were sufficiently potent so as to override the effect of the hyperglycaemia. They held that stress, anxiety and depression could be caused by external factors but are not themselves external factors within the meaning of the law. The Court considered that they constitute a state of mind which is likely to recur – that being the basis of the distinction between insane and non-insane automatism in the caselaw.

So it is that the 'internal' / 'external' distinction has led to the legally sound, but logically obscure, decisions that a man in a state of hypoglycaemia was suffering from non-insane automatism and a man in a state of hyperglycaemia was legally insane. Both men were diabetics, and there is nothing to say that either condition was at greater risk of recurrence than the other. After all, Quick's condition could recur should he fail once again to eat enough food. Hennessy's condition could recur should he have failed once again to take enough insulin.

Only a few years before the case of _Hennessy_, the Court of Appeal considered the case of _Bailey_ (1983) 1 WLR 760. Mr Bailey had attacked another man with an iron bar and faced a charge of wounding with intent. In his defence Mr Bailey – who was a diabetic – claimed that at the time of the event he was in a hypoglycaemic state, caused by his failure to eat sufficient food after a dose of insulin. At trial, the Judge directed the jury to disregard the automatism defence as it did not apply to self-induced incapacity.

The Court of Appeal held that self-induced incapacity may in fact provide a defence to crimes of basic intent, as well as specific intent, where the prosecution could not prove the necessary element of recklessness.

Where a person is aware of the negative effects of taking in a particular substance, they are reckless in taking the substance anyway. For that reason, they will have no defence to crimes of basic intent, which do not require a specific intent to commit an offence but simply a recklessness as to whether it will be committed. However, if the person is unaware of the potential negative effects then the necessary recklessness is not proven.

The Court in *Bailey* had the following to say on the subject at 764 to 765:

> *"It is common knowledge that those who take alcohol to excess or certain sorts of drugs may become aggressive or do dangerous or unpredictable things, they may be able to foresee the risks of causing harm to others but nevertheless persist in their conduct. But the same cannot be said without more of a man who fails to take food after an insulin injection. If he does appreciate the risk that such a failure may lead to aggressive, unpredictable and uncontrollable conduct and he nevertheless deliberately runs the risk or otherwise disregards it, this will amount to recklessness. But we certainly do not think that it is common knowledge, even among diabetics, that such is a consequence of a failure to take food and there is no evidence that it was known to this appellant. Doubtless he knew that if he failed to take his insulin or proper food after it he might lose consciousness, but as such he would only be a danger to himself unless he put himself in charge of some machine such as a motor car, which required his continued conscious control.*
>
> *In our judgment, self-induced automatism, other than that due to intoxication from alcohol or drugs, may provide a defence to crimes of basic intent. The question in each case will be whether the prosecution have proved the necessary element of recklessness. In cases of assault, if the accused knows that his actions or inaction are likely to make him aggressive, unpredictable or uncontrolled with the result that he may cause some injury to others and he persists in the action or takes no remedial action when he knows it is required, it will be open to the jury to find that he was reckless."*

Incidentally, it so happened that in Bailey's particular case, the Court found that even had the jury been properly directed, they would have rejected his defence on the factual basis. There was substantial evidence that he had armed himself purposefully to carry out the attack. On that basis, then, the appeal was dismissed.

In the case of _C_ (2007) EWCA Crim 1862, the Court of Appeal held that it was for the defence to provide a sufficient evidential foundation to allow the defence of non-insane automatism to be open to the jury. That evidence was evidence of a total loss of control. The evidence as to the blood sugar level of the appellant was not in itself evidence of a total loss of control because only the appellant could say what was in his mind at the relevant time. Therefore, the judge's decision to allow a submission of no case to answer was held to be premature where it was not established whether there was a sufficient evidential basis for the defence.

Finally, the relatively more recent case of _De Boise_ (2014) EWCA Crim 1121 – whilst dismissing the appeal for various reasons – considered the fact that the expert evidence in that case raised no more than a possibility that the appellant was suffering from a hypoglycaemic attack at the time. The Court remarked that it will look for more than a 'mere possibility'.

The effect of both _C_ and _De Boise_ is to make clear that there is a real and significant burden on the defence to raise a sufficient evidential foundation to justify leaving the defence of non-insane automatism to the jury. It will not be enough to merely advance the idea that the defendant was in such a state.

CHAPTER SEVEN

SPECIAL CASES – SLEEPWALKING

THE DIFFICULTY WITH SLEEPWALKING – A COMPARISON OF TWO JURISDICTIONS

The way in which the criminal justice system treats sleepwalking is far from clear. In order to undertake a proper analysis of sleepwalking in the criminal law, we must go across the pond to Canada, home to the 1992 Canadian Supreme Court case of Kenneth Parks – perhaps the most well-known case of a crime committed whilst sleepwalking.

Kenneth Parks was a married man, with a history of sleepwalking. At the time of the incident in question, he had been under extreme financial stress.

One night in 1987, Kenneth Parks rose from his bed, walked out of his house, got into his car and drove 23 km to the home of his parents-in-law. Once inside their house, he armed himself with a kitchen knife and brutally attacked his parents-in-law. The attack was so severe that it left his mother-in-law dead, and his father-in-law badly injured.

He went to the police station covered in blood and told them he thought he had done something horrible.

At trial, the Judge determined that – on the evidence – Mr Parks had been sleepwalking and that this was properly characterised as simple automatism.

The Prosecution duly appealed to the Court of Appeal, and to the Supreme Court of Canada, on the basis that sleepwalking is more appropriately characterised as a form of insane automatism. This argument was dismissed by both higher Courts. The Supreme Court of Canada analysed the principles to be followed when considering whether a condition is to be categorised as insane or non-insane automatism (*Parks* (1992) 2 SCR 871). In the decision *per* La Forest, L'Heureux-Dubé and Gonthier JJ:

> "*When a defence of non-insane automatism is raised by the accused, the trial judge must determine whether the defence should be left with the trier of fact. This will involve two discrete tasks. First, he or she must determine whether there is some evidence on the record to support leaving the defence with the jury. An evidential burden rests with the accused; the mere assertion of the defence will not suffice.*
>
> *Given the proper foundation, the trial judge must then consider whether the condition alleged by the accused is, in law, non-insane automatism. If the trial judge is satisfied that there is some evidence pointing to a condition that is in law non-insane automatism, then the defence can be left with the jury.*
>
> *[...]*
>
> *Two distinct approaches to the policy component of insanity have emerged in automatism cases, the "continuing danger" and "internal cause" theories. The first theory holds that any condition likely to present recurring danger should be treated as insanity. The second holds that a condition stemming from the internal make-up of the accused, rather than external factors, should lead to a finding of insanity. Though seemingly divergent, both theories stem from a concern for the protection of the public.*
>
> *Though the second theory has gained a certain ascendency, it is merely an analytical tool and is not universal. In particular, it is not helpful in assessing the nature of a somnambulistic condition. The distinction between internal and external causes is blurred*

during sleep, and certain causes that are discounted for a subject who is awake may have entirely different effects on a sleeping person. As for the "continuing danger" test, it has been criticized as a general theory. However, the purpose of the insanity defence has always been the protection of the public against recurrent danger. As such, the possibility of recurrence, though not determinative, may be looked upon as a factor at the policy stage of the inquiry on the issue of insanity."

The key points to take from this decision are that: a) the Court held that the 'internal'/'external' test is not helpful when applied to actions committed whilst sleepwalking; b) the primary purpose of the law of automatism is protection of the public; c) the danger of recurrence is a factor to be taken into account.

On the evidence in *Parks*, there was no likelihood of recurrence and no compelling policy factors to preclude a defence of non-insane automatism.

Around the same time as the Supreme Court was conducting its landmark analysis, the England and Wales Court of Criminal Appeal was conducting the same analysis in the case of *Burgess* (1991) 2 QB 92. The interesting point is that there were remarkable similarities between the approaches of the two courts, but they diverged into two completely opposing conclusions.

The Supreme Court in *Parks* held that there was a two-step test for the trial judge faced with a defence of automatism: (i) to determine whether there is some evidence to support leaving the defence with the jury; (ii) to determine whether the condition is, in law, non-insane automatism.

Having concluded that the evidential burden had been met in that case, the Supreme Court then went on to conclude that sleepwalking was a non-insane automatism as a matter of law.

The Court of Appeal in _Burgess_ held (at 96) that there was a two-step test for the trial judge faced with such a defence: (i) to determine whether a proper evidential foundation had been laid for the defence; (ii) to determine whether the evidence showed the case to be one of insane or non-insane automatism.

The facts in _Burgess_ were as follows. In the early hours of 12 June 1988, Mr Burgess and his friend were asleep in the same residence. Whilst his friend was asleep, Mr Burgess viciously and suddenly attacked her with a bottle, then a video recorder and finally grasping her around the throat. Mr Burgess claimed that he was asleep at the time, and so had not known what he was doing nor had he formed the intention required.

The trial judge held that Mr Burgess had raised a defence of insane automatism, following which the jury found him not guilty by reason of insanity. Burgess appealed on the basis that the judge had erred in rejecting the submission that he was suffering from sane automatism.

Having set out the two-step test at 96, the Court of Appeal then turned its focus to the 'internal'/'external' doctrine to assist it in answering the difficult question of categorisation:

> "_The appellant plainly suffered from a defect of reason from some sort of failure (for lack of a better term) of the mind causing him to act as he did without conscious motivation. His mind was to some extent controlling his actions which were purposive rather than the result simply of muscular spasm, but without his being consciously aware of what he was doing. Can it be said that that "failure" was a disease of the mind rather than a defect or failure of the mind not due to disease? That is the distinction, by no means always easy to draw, upon which this case depends, as others have depended in the past._

One can perhaps narrow the field of inquiry still further by eliminating what are sometimes called the "external factors" such as concussion caused by a blow on the head. There were no such factors here. Whatever the cause may have been, it was an "internal" cause."

Unlike the Canadian court, the court in *Burgess* felt able to definitively state that the cause of the appellant's acts were internal.

Additionally, the Court in *Burgess* placed different weight on the possibility of recurrence than did the Supreme Court of Canada. In their reasoning, it was no more than a supportive factor for a decision to categorise a defence as one of insanity. At 99:

"It seems to us that if there is a danger of recurrence that may be an added reason for categorising the condition as a disease of the mind. On the other hand, the absence of the danger of recurrence is not a reason for saying that it cannot be a disease of the mind."

By contrast, the Supreme Court of Canada appears to have placed the possibility of recurrence at the forefront of its reasoning.

It is difficult to criticise the reasoning in either case. There are persuasive grounds for arguing that sleepwalking should be classed as a non-insane automatism, given the lack of danger of recurrence and the fact that it can be triggered by both an internal proclivity to sleepwalk and external triggers. Similarly, the Court in *Burgess* make persuasive arguments for leaving the practical consideration of danger of recurrence towards the tail end of analysis of legal principles. It is also right that sleepwalking can be said to be distinct from a concussion, a bee-sting or other such external factor.

The overarching point is that neither conclusion satisfactorily fits the phenomenon of sleepwalking. Whilst a person may be more prone to sleepwalking, it is settled medical doctrine that they may not sleepwalk unless subject to triggers such as caffeine, alcohol, external stresses, lack of sleep and so on. Whilst a number of people may sleepwalk, they do not all commit violent or criminal acts while sleepwalking. The legal precedent reveals no separate medical condition of 'violent somnambulism'. The reality seems to be that it is a variety of factors that may combine to result in criminal acts whilst asleep. Such a complex phenomenon may not, it seems, lend itself easily to one category or the other.

A STUDY OF SLEEPWALKING CASES IN ENGLAND AND WALES

The difficulty with classifying sleepwalking is all too apparent when we consider the various ways in which the criminal courts in England and Wales have dealt with the defence over the last twenty years.

In 2002, the guitarist Peter Buck, of rock band REM, found himself relying on the automatism defence. He attacked British Airways staff whilst on a transatlantic flight to London. At the start of the flight, he had taken a sleeping pill and drunk some wine. His defence was that he was in a somnambulistic state; the medical evidence supported this. Mr Buck was acquitted of the attack on the basis of non-insane automatism.

After a night out in 2005, James Bilton and a female acquaintance decided to sleep the evening off at his flat. The woman slept in the bed whilst Mr Bilton slept on the sofa. However, in the middle of the night, the woman woke to find that Mr Bilton was having sex with her. At trial, Mr Bilton (who had a history of sleepwalking) claimed that he was completely oblivious to what actually happened, and had committed the acts in his sleep. In December 2005 Mr Bilton was acquitted of three counts of rape at York Crown Court on the basis that he was suffering from non-insane automatism.

That same year, James Lowe beat his 83-year old father to death in a seemingly unmotivated attack. On 18 March 2005 he was found not

SPECIAL CASES – SLEEPWALKING

guilty by reason of insanity, after the jury accepted that he was sleepwalking at the time.

In 2006, Christopher Davies faced a trial for sexual assault. The victim claimed that she fell asleep on the floor of a friend's home after a party. She woke to find Mr Davies sexually assaulting her. Mr Davies accepted that he committed the actions but said that it must have happened in his sleep. Expert evidence was called to support his defence. In summing up, the Judge told the jury that sleepwalking was recognised as a total destruction of voluntary control, and if that was what happened, Mr Davies should be found not guilty. Mr Davies was subsequently acquitted.

In 2007, David Pooley faced trial for raping a woman on his RAF base. He claimed that he had no recollection of the time and had a history of sleepwalking since his childhood. A neurologist specialising in parasomniac behaviours was called to support the defence of sleepwalking. Mr Pooley was acquitted on the basis that he had been suffering non-insane automatism at the time.

In 2009, Brian Thomas appeared in court for the murder of his wife. He had strangled his wife one night when they were camping in Wales. By all accounts, the pair were a loving couple with no significant problems. Mr Thomas claimed that he had been asleep at the time. Medical evidence – including sleep studies performed on him whilst he was on remand in prison – supported his account. In this case, the Prosecution accepted Mr Thomas' account but had initially submitted that the only defence raised was one of insane automatism. Upon reviewing the case, the Prosecution determined that no useful purpose could be served by a hospital order and so decided to offer no evidence.

Most recently, in 2019 Dale Kelly faced trial for sexual assault. After a night out with a friend and that friend's girlfriend, the three slept in one residence. The woman woke up in the night to find that Mr Kelly had sexually assaulted her. Mr Kelly claimed that he was sleeping at the time. Medical evidence indicated that he suffered from sleepwalking. Mr Kelly was found not guilty by reason of insanity.

This catalogue of first-instance decisions indicates that there has been no uniform way that the courts have approached sleepwalking. Without being able to analyse the specific directions and any legal submissions in each case, it is not possible to determine whether the different features of the case justify the different approaches. It is not clear the extent to which there was preliminary legal argument as to whether the acts, if proven, amounted to insane or non-insane automatism. The only thing that is clear is that there is room for the practitioner to argue persuasively for either categorisation. Given the lack of clarity, it would seem imperative that the way in which the Judge will direct the jury should be discussed between counsel and the bench at as early a stage as possible, so as to avoid ambiguity as the trial progresses.

CHAPTER EIGHT

SPECIAL CASES – INTOXICATION

A BACKGROUND TO INTOXICATION

The use of intoxication as a defence is heavily restricted, for good policy reasons. The consequences of freely allowing intoxication to be a legal justification are not difficult to imagine. By the same token, there should be recognition that in some circumstances a person should not be held responsible for their actions when under the influence of alcohol or another psychoactive substance.

The courts have tended to pose three key questions when determining whether intoxication can form a defence.

(i) Is the defendant's intoxication voluntary or involuntary? If the latter, it may be a defence;

(ii) If the intoxication is voluntary, is the crime charged one of 'specific' intent or 'basic' intent? If the former, then voluntary intoxication may be a defence;

(iii) If the crime is one of basic intent, is the drug involved one known to create states of unpredictability or aggression? If the answer is no – i.e. the defendant took a drug without realising that it could cause unpredictability or aggression – then it may be a defence.

The development of the caselaw in relation to intoxication in general merits consideration. In <u>Attorney-General for Northern Ireland v Gallagher</u> (1963) AC 349, the appellant had been convicted of murdering his wife whilst in a psychopathic rage precipitated by his drinking whisky. The House of Lords considered the case before them against:

> "...*the general principle of English law that, subject to very limited exceptions, drunkenness is no defence to a criminal charge, nor is a defect of reason produced by drunkenness. This principle was stated by Sir Matthew Hale in his Pleas of the Crown, I, p. 32, in words which I would repeat here:* "This vice" (drunkenness) "doth deprive men of the use of reason, and puts many men into a perfect, but temporary phrenzy ... By the laws of England such a person shall have no privilege by this voluntary contracted madness, but shall have the same judgment as if he were in his right senses."

Their Lordships then continued to consider the various ways in which drunkenness might impair a person's power of reason:

(i) It may impair a person's power of perception and so ability to foresee the consequences of their action. Nevertheless, the person is not allowed to use their self-induced want of perception as a defence;

(ii) It may impair a person's power to judge between right or wrong, so that they do things while drunk that they would not dream of doing when sober. Nevertheless, the person cannot use their self-induced want of moral sense as a defence;

(iii) It may impair a person's power of self-control so that they more readily give way to provocation than if sober. Nevertheless, the person cannot use their self-induced want of self-control as a defence.

Their Lordships proceeded to say that the general principle, however, is subject to the following exceptions:

SPECIAL CASES – INTOXICATION

(i) If a person is charged with an offence in which a specific intent is essential, then evidence of drunkenness that rendered them incapable of forming that specific intent is an answer. This degree of drunkenness is where a person is rendered so stupid by drink that they do not know what they are doing. Their Lordships quoted cases where a drunken nurse put a baby in a fire, mistaking the baby for a log of wood, and where a drunken man thought his friend in bed was a theatrical dummy and stabbed it to death.

(ii) If a person by drinking brings on a distinct disease of the mind, such as delirium tremens, so that he is temporarily insane within the M'Naghten Rules then he has a defence on the grounds of insanity.

At 382 and 383, the law was summarised as follows:

"My Lords, I think the law on this point should take a clear stand. If a man, whilst sane and sober, forms an intention to kill and makes preparation for it, knowing it is a wrong thing to do, and then gets himself drunk so as to give himself Dutch courage to do the killing, and whilst drunk carries out his intention, he cannot rely on this self-induced drunkenness as a defence to a charge of murder, nor even as reducing it to manslaughter. He cannot say that he got himself into such a stupid state that he was incapable of an intent to kill. So also when he is a psychopath, he cannot by drinking rely on his self-induced defect of reason as a defence of insanity. The wickedness of his mind before he got drunk is enough to condemn him, coupled with the act which he intended to do and did do. A psychopath who goes out intending to kill, knowing it is wrong, and does kill, cannot escape the consequences by making himself drunk before doing it.

[...]

> *I would agree, of course, that if before the killing he had discarded his intention to kill or reversed it – and then got drunk – it would be a different matter. But when he forms the intention to kill and without interruption proceeds to get drunk and carry out his intention, then his drunkenness is no defence and nonetheless so because it is dressed up as a defence of insanity. There was no evidence in this case of any interruption and there was no need for the Lord Chief Justice to mention it to the jury.*
>
> *I need hardly say, of course, that I have here only considered the law of Northern Ireland. In England a psychopath such as this man might now be in a position to raise a defence of diminished responsibility under section 2 of the Homicide Act, 1957."*

In *Sheehan* (1975) 2 All ER 960, the Court of Appeal set out guidance as to the proper direction to give to a jury where intoxication was said to have had an influence on intention. At 744:

> *"… in cases where drunkenness and its possible effect upon the defendant's mens rea is an issue, we think that the proper direction to a jury is, first, to warn them that the mere fact that the defendant's mind was affected by drink so that he acted in a way in which he would not have done had he been sober does not assist him at all, provided that the necessary intention was there. A drunken intent is nevertheless an intent. Secondly, and subject to this, the jury should merely be instructed to have regard to all the evidence, including that relating to drink, to draw such inferences as they think proper from the evidence, and on that basis to ask themselves whether they feel sure that at the material time the defendant had the requisite intent."*

The key question, then, is whether the defendant had the requisite intent. The reason why – i.e. the fact that he only formed the intent because he was drunk – is irrelevant. Alcohol may only be relevant as one of the factors that a jury could take into account in order to determine whether the defendant had the requisite intent at the relevant time.

The House of Lords in _DPP v Majewski_ (1977) AC 443 provided further elaboration on the comments of the Court in _Gallagher_ about intoxication as a defence to crimes of specific intent.

In _Majewski_ the defendant had assaulted a number of police officers when he was being restrained and arrested. He had taken a combination of drink and drugs and was heavily intoxicated. He claimed that his self-induced intoxication prevented him from forming the intention. He was convicted. The case made its way to the House of Lords, who upheld the conviction. At 476:

> "...*if there is a substantive rule of law that in crimes of basic intent, the factor of intoxication is irrelevant (and such I hold to be the substantive law), evidence with regard to it is quite irrelevant.*
>
> *[...]*
>
> *My noble and learned friends and I think it may be helpful if we give the following indication of the general lines on which in our view the jury should be directed as to the effect upon the criminal responsibility of the accused of drink or drugs or both, whenever death or physical injury to another person results from something done by the accused for which there is no legal justification and the offence with which the accused is charged is manslaughter or assault at common law or the statutory offence of unlawful wounding under section 20 , or of assault occasioning actual bodily harm under section 47 of the Offences against the Person Act 1861 .*
>
> *In the case of these offences it is no excuse in law that, because of drink or drugs which the accused himself had taken knowingly and willingly, he had deprived himself of the ability to exercise self-control, to realise the possible consequences of what he was doing, or even to be conscious that he was doing it. As in the instant case, the*

> *jury may be properly instructed that they "can ignore the subject of drink or drugs as being in any way a defence" to charges of this character."*

More recently, the cases of *Mohamadi* (2020) EWCA Crim 327 and *Campaneu* (2020) EWCA Crim 362 emphasised that the question is whether the accused in fact formed the intention, not whether he was capable of so doing.

THE RELATIONSHIP BETWEEN INTOXICATION AND INSANITY

In *Coley* (2013) EWCA Crim 223, the Court drew a distinction between being drunk and suffering from a disease of the mind.

The appellant was charged with attempted murder. One evening he had dressed up in combat gear and broken into his neighbour's house. He was carrying what was described as a 'Rambo knife'. He stabbed his neighbour repeatedly and then escaped from the house.

The appellant claimed that he had no recollection of the stabbing. He was a heavy cannabis user. Three experts testified that whilst he was not suffering from an underlying mental illness, there was a real possibility that he had suffered a brief psychotic episode induced by the cannabis. The trial Judge declined to leave either insanity or automatism to the jury, and the appellant was convicted.

The Court of Appeal, dismissing the appeal, held (at paragraphs 17 to 18):

> *"...the law has to cope with the synthesising of the law of insanity with the law of voluntary intoxication. The first calls for a special verdict of acquittal and very particular means of disposal. The latter is generally no defence at all, but may be relevant to whether the defendant formed a specific intention, if the offence in question is one which requires such: DPP v Majewski [1977] AC 443 . In*

SPECIAL CASES – INTOXICATION

most, but not all, intoxication cases, the intoxication will be possibly relevant to a serious offence allegedly committed but will afford no defence to a lesser offence constituted by the same facts: for example causing grievous bodily harm with intent (s 18) and causing grievous bodily harm without such intent (s20), or of course murder and manslaughter. In the development of the common law, intoxication was historically regarded chiefly as an aggravation of offending, rather than as an excuse for it. For all the reasons explained in Majewski , the law refuses as a matter of policy to afford a general defence to an offender on the basis of his own voluntary intoxication. The pressing social reasons for maintaining this general policy of the law are certainly no less present in modern conditions of substance abuse than they were in the past.

18. The precise line between the law of voluntary intoxication and the law of insanity may, we do not doubt, be difficult to identify in some borderline cases. But the present case falls comfortably on the side of the line covered by voluntary intoxication. It matters not that the condition of the defendant as observed in the aftermath of his attack on the neighbour was not that of conventional intoxication, in the sense that he was not, for example, staggering or unable to speak clearly. If the doctors were right about his state of mind, his mind was to an extent detached from reality by the direct and acute effects on it of the ingestion of cannabis. Every intoxicated person has his mind affected, and to an extent disordered, by the direct and acute effects of the ingestion of intoxicants; all intoxication operates through the brain. Not infrequently it would be perfectly legitimate to say of a very drunken man that his mind had become detached from reality by the intoxication; that is obviously true, for example, of the drunken man who suffers delusions as a result of the drink, but the proposition is not limited to that case. In order to engage the law of insanity, it is not enough that there is an effect on the mind, or, in the language of the M'Naghten rules, a 'defect of reason'. There must also be what the law classifies as a disease of the mind.

67

Direct acute effects on the mind of intoxicants, voluntarily taken, are not so classified."

It is clear, then, that the effects on the mind of intoxicants such as alcohol or cannabis will not reach the standard of 'disease of the mind'. However, consider the case where the accused is not intoxicated at the time but suffers from a recognised medical condition as a result of extensive abuse of intoxicants.

This was the case in *Harris*, conjoined with *Coley* on appeal. In that case, the appellant was in the habit of binge drinking for several days at a time. After a week of so doing, he took time to sober up before returning to work. However, several days later he set fire to his home. He was charged with aggravated arson. His denied culpability as he claimed that his psychosis made him give no thought at all as to risk caused to others, and on that basis he was not reckless. His defence was not based on intoxication at the time of the event, as he was in fact sober at the time. Instead, his defence was that his chronic alcohol abuse had caused a disease of the mind in the form of alcoholic psychosis. It was accepted at trial that he was in fact suffering a psychotic episode at the time of the event. The trial judge ruled that he would direct the jury to consider the appellant's actions as if he had not been drinking. Consequently, the appellant pleaded guilty and appealed on the basis that he ought to have had the chance to advance his defence before the jury. The Court of Appeal allowed his appeal. At paragraphs 59 to 60:

"59. The argument for the Crown in this case is that the mental illness from which the defendant was suffering was brought on by his past voluntary drinking. Therefore, it is contended, it should be treated in the same way as if he were still drunk. We agree that there is scope for the argument that an illness caused by his own fault ought as a matter of policy to be treated in the same way as is drunkenness at the time of the offence. This would, however, represent a significant extension of DPP v Majewski and of the

> *similar principle expounded in Quick, which likewise concerned a case where what was asserted was an acute condition (there of automatism) induced arguably by the defendant's fault. A great many mental illnesses have their roots in culpable past misconduct of the sufferer: those attributable to many years of past drug or alcohol abuse are perhaps the most obvious, but there could be many other examples, such as perhaps a culpable failure to follow a recommended medical regime, or maybe the consequences of traumatic brain injury caused by one's own drunken driving. Whether the Majewski approach ought to be extended to such cases may be a topic which might be addressed in the forthcoming work of the Law Commission on loss of capacity, and it should, no doubt, be the subject of proper public debate. But in the present state of the law, Majewski applies to offences committed by persons who are then voluntarily intoxicated but not to those who are suffering mental illness. This defendant was, it is clear, suffering from a condition of mental illness when he set fire to his own house. That it was not long-lasting does not mean that it was not a true illness. In our view he was entitled to have tried the question of whether, in the condition in which he was, he was actually aware of the risk which he created for his neighbours.*
>
> *60. It follows that we grant Harris leave to appeal against conviction, allow the appeal and quash his conviction."*

Although the particular case of Harris did not involve a plea of insane automatism, it is not difficult to envisage a situation where such a plea would be advanced. Should a defendant suffer a severe psychosis or similar brought on by chronic substance abuse which rendered him unable to know what he was doing or to differentiate right from wrong, the remarks of the Court of Appeal indicate that he may be entitled to leave the defence of insanity to the jury. This proposition finds support in the remarks of their Lordships in the case of *Gallagher*, to the effect that a disorder of the mind brought on by alcohol abuse would provide the accused with a defence under the M'Naghten Rules.

It should be noted that an accused need not have consumed alcohol immediately before the relevant event in order to have acted in a way attributable to intoxication. The Court of Appeal in *Taj* (2018) EWCA Crim 1743 considered section 76(5) of the Criminal Justice and Immigration Act 2008, which precluded a defendant from relying on self-defence based on a mistaken belief where that belief was 'attributable to intoxication'. The Court held that the section did not merely cover cases where alcohol or drugs were still present in the defendant's system. They could cover a state of mind "*immediately and proximately*" based on earlier drinking or drug-taking. However, the Court of Appeal did make clear that such an interpretation did not extend to long-term mental illness due to alcohol or drug misuse. It seems that in the latter situation the insanity defence would still apply.

CHAPTER NINE

SPECIAL CASES – DISCRETE SITUATIONS

PRE-MENSTRUAL SYNDROME

There have been some cases where severe pre-menstrual syndrome has amounted to an explanation for committing an offence.

The case of Sandie Craddock (*Craddock* (1980) 5 WLUK 3) concerned a woman who was convicted of stabbing a colleague to death. She was 28 years of age, and had 30 convictions, primarily for criminal damage and assault. She had made numerous attempts at suicide. Various types of sentence had been tried. She had been examined by psychiatrists, who had formed the view that she suffered from no mental illness.

As it happened, her father noticed that all the offences happened in 28-day cycles. Testing was undertaken which revealed that she suffered from a progesterone deficiency that led to a severe hormonal imbalance. Accordingly, her sentence was deferred for three months to allow her to undertake progesterone treatment. The results were excellent: her personality completely stabilised and it was considered that it would continue to remain stable whilst she continued the treatment. The court heard submissions about the nature and impact of pre-menstrual syndrome. Ms Craddock was sentenced to an order in the community as a result.

The case of Christine English at Norwich Crown Court in 1981 is a similar example. Ms English drove her car at her lover, crushing him to death. On 10 November 1981, she was given a conditional discharge and a ban from driving, on the basis that she was suffering from pre-menstrual syndrome at the time.

More recently, in 2018 the High Court in Rajasthan, India, acquitted a woman of murder of her baby after finding that she was suffering from a form of mental disorder brought on by her pre-menstrual syndrome.

It is right to say that such cases are rarely argued. There may be a general unease around such a submission. The Courts have remarked on the apparent incongruity of labelling a sleepwalker 'insane' (_Burgess_). The same may be said for claiming that a woman has less control over herself during her monthly cycle, even if the argument does not go so far as to claim she is legally insane. The English cases in the 1980s led to sensationalist headlines centred around the idea of hormonal women. The Indian court's decision has been simultaneously applauded for its recognition of the very real struggles faced by the defendant, and criticised for advancing a narrative of a hormonal, hysterical woman.

Without more reported cases, it is difficult to gauge how such a claim might be treated by the courts of England and Wales now, some forty years after the cases of _Craddock_ and _English_. However, it is worth being aware that pre-menstrual syndrome has been found to mitigate culpability in the past, and might do so again.

UNDIAGNOSED SLEEP APNOEA

Sleep apnoea is a condition of varying levels of severity, which causes the sufferer to have disturbed sleep due to difficulties breathing whilst asleep. It is easily treated, using a CPAP machine to assist the sufferer during the night.

However, untreated sleep apnoea can lead to extreme fatigue. Studies have shown that people with undiagnosed sleep apnoea are at greater risk of falling asleep at the wheel. Of course, this could be extremely dangerous – not simply for the driver but for others on the road.

A person facing charges of causing death or serious injury by driving will not be able to escape liability for falling asleep at the wheel. The law generally takes the view that the person was reckless in driving when so tired, in the same way that a person who has imbibed alcohol might be. However, what of the situation where a person has in fact fallen asleep due to an undiagnosed medical condition such as sleep apnoea?

We have seen that it is settled law that a person cannot be conscious of what they are doing if they are asleep. We have also seen that it is settled law that a person who is responsible for their lack of awareness (such as where they drink alcohol) cannot then escape responsibility. If a person was not responsible for their lack of consciousness, because their condition was undiagnosed, then it follows that they must have a defence to any criminal action. This would accord with the Court of Appeal decisions we considered in relation to diabetes. In those cases, the Court emphasised that the appellants were unaware of the effect that lack of food or too little insulin would have on their reactions. The implication is that if they had been so aware, they would not have been able to put forward a defence.

PSYCHOLOGICAL BLOW

In the Canadian case of _Rabey_ (1977) 37 CCC (2d), the court considered whether a psychological blow could be so severe as to render the accused in a state of automatism. In that case, the accused was a student who was infatuated with a girl. When he discovered that the girl did not return his feelings, he reacted violently, hitting her over the head with a rock. He was acquitted of causing bodily harm with intent on the ground of automatism. The trial judge accepted that he was in a dissociative state caused by the psychological blow of his rejection. The trial judge held that the psychological blow was an external factor analogous to a blow to the skull that caused concussion.

The Ontario Court of Appeal allowed the prosecution's appeal. The case then made its way to the Supreme Court who, similarly, rejected the trial judge's reasoning. They endorsed the view of the Court of Appeal that the *"ordinary stresses and disappointments of life which are the common lot of mankind do not constitute an external cause ..."*. The extraordinary effect which the ordinary event had on the accused had its root in his emotional or psychological make-up.

There does not appear to have been any such argument made before the courts of England and Wales. I am doubtful that such an argument would find any traction. A large number of defendants in the criminal courts for offences of violence have been triggered by emotional events and that is rarely an excuse. If there was compelling expert evidence to the effect that the accused suffered from a mental disease which was triggered by such a rejection, that might have some relevance – but that would be based upon the underlying mental disorder rather than the rejection itself.

CHAPTER TEN

SCOPE FOR REFORM?

Throughout this book, we have seen cracks in the law of insane and non-insane automatism. There are circumstances where the strict application of the law does not seem to accord with either logic or medical sense. It is worth considering possible criticisms of the law as it stands today.

First, there are questions as to whether the 'internal' / 'external' distinction is fit for purpose. As noted at the start of this book, a focus on whether a condition is caused by an internal or an external factor suits those cases that fall at either end of the spectrum. A blow to the head causing a concussion is undoubtedly an external factor. A long-lasting mental health condition is undoubtedly an internal factor. The reality, though, is that there are numerous human conditions which do not fit neatly into one mould or the other.

Sleepwalking is an example which straddles both. A tendency to sleepwalk could be said to be an internal issue: some people are simply more predisposed to sleepwalk. However, the triggers for sleepwalking can be found in external causes. So it is that caffeine, external stress factors, issues causing lack of sleep and alcohol can trigger a person into a somnambulistic state. Violence whilst sleepwalking may also be caused by an external factor. A sleepwalker disturbed by another person may react violently; they will not seek out a person to be violent towards. Thus that interruption is the external trigger that causes the violence.

The chapter on diabetes presented us with other examples of the difficulties caused when reliant on the 'internal'/'external' distinction. Failure to take insulin, and so regulate the body's natural production of insulin, has been held to constitute an internal factor – as it is the body's production of insulin that is at fault. Conversely, taking too much insulin has been held to be an external factor, as it is the medicine itself that has caused the automatism.

Secondly, there are problems with focusing on the possibility of recurrence. In <u>Burgess</u>, the Court of Appeal indicated that the possibility of recurrence may be an additional factor in categorising something as insanity but is not in itself decisive. This makes sense in principle, as an over-reliance on the possibility of recurrence in particular cases could lead to different people with the same medical condition being categorised entirely differently. The lack of certainty that would cause would not be desirable at all. Equally it would sit at odds with the rest of the criminal law, where the possibility that an accused may go on to commit further crimes is normally only taken into account at sentencing stage.

Thirdly, there may be problems with the interpretation of 'disease of the mind' as a legal concept with lack of direct correlation with medical terms. Article 5(1)(e) of the European Convention on Human Rights provides:

> *"(1) Everyone has the right to liberty and security of person. No one shall be deprived of his liberty save in the following cases and in accordance with a procedure prescribed by law:*
>
> *[...]*
>
> *(e) the lawful detention of persons for the prevention of the spreading of infectious diseases, of persons of unsound mind, alcoholics or drug addicts or vagrants..."*

The European case of <u>Winterwerp v Netherlands</u> (1979) 2 EHRR 387 held that there must be objective medical expertise supporting the fact that the accused is of unsound mind. The case of <u>Varbanov v Bulgaria</u> (5 October 2000, Application No. 31365/96) held that the medical assessment must be based on the actual state of the mental health of the person concerned and not solely on past events. A medical opinion could not be sufficient to justify deprivation of liberty if a significant period of time has elapsed.

The defence of insanity, by its nature, rests on the state of the accused's mind at the time of the commission of the offence. This may well mean that a significant period of time has elapsed.

Of course, before imposing a hospital order, it may be that the court satisfies this apparent incongruity by ordering psychiatric reports as to the accused's current state of mind. However, on its face, the fact that the insanity defence could lead to deprivation of liberty means that there is seemingly a disconnect between that process and the rights guaranteed by Article 5 of the European Convention on Human Rights.

In 2013, the Law Commission published a report: *Criminal Liability: Insanity and Automatism*.

At paragraph 1.40, the Commission noted that the broad interpretation of 'disease of the mind' has meant that people with conditions that would not ordinarily be described as mental disorders have been described as 'insane' for the purposes of the M'Naghten Rules. At paragraph 1.41, the Commission attributes this to the 'internal'/'external' method of categorising the accused's condition.

The principal proposal from the Law Commission was to replace the common law insanity defence with a new statutory defence. This defence would hold that a person can be held not to be criminally responsible by reason of a qualifying recognised medical condition. The party seeking to raise the defence would need to adduce expert evidence that at the time of the offence the defendant wholly lacked one of the following capacities:

    (i)   To make a judgment rationally;

(ii) To understand that they are doing something wrong; or

(iii) To control their actions.

Not all medical conditions would qualify. The Commission takes the view that as a mater of policy, not all recognised medical conditions should qualify as a 'recognised medical condition'. One example would be acute intoxication.

The Law Commission proposed further reforms to the existing law of non-insane automatism. Again, the common law defence would be replaced with a statutory defence, available where the accused had a total loss of control other than one arising from a recognised medical condition. That would likely only apply in a discrete number of cases. Such an example might be the rare case where a swarm of bees flies into a car window, confusing the driver such that he is no longer in control of his actions.

CONCLUSION: PRACTICAL TIPS

I began this book by referring to the fact that cases of insane and non-insane automatism will not form the 'bread and butter' of the average criminal practitioner. However, the cases set out in this book indicate that the defence is raised more often than may be thought at first blush. I hope that this book has provided you with an understanding of the issues to consider when that case lands on your desk. This final chapter will set out a checklist of practical tips for you to follow. They act as guidance only, and you may wish to add to them or detract from them as you see fit. The points below are adaptable to both the defence and the prosecution.

- Determine whether the accused has raised an issue of automatism. Not all accused will be aware that they have in fact raised such a defence. For example, the diabetic person who says their memory is blurry may not necessarily link that to the lack of food they ate after their insulin injection.

- Consider whether voluntary intoxication forms any part of the case. If so, then the principles in relation to intoxication should be closely considered, by reference to whether the crime is one of specific or basic intent and whether the substance ingested is one known to create states of automatism.

- Consider who should be the appropriate expert(s) in your particular case. A case involving sleepwalking will likely need a specific specialist on sleep, for example. A case involving diabetes can be dealt with by a more general medical expert.

- Consider whether legal precedent indicates that the defence is one of insane or non-insane automatism. Remember that the issue may not be clear-cut in the caselaw, such as in the case of sleepwalking.

- Remember that if the defence raised is one of insane automatism, the defence will need to provide the evidence of two or more registered practitioners, at least one of whom is 'duly approved'.

- In cases that do not clearly fall within insane or non-insane automatism, consider the particular features of your case such as the possibility of recurrence and the specific trigger for the actions.

- Consider whether there will need to be legal argument at an early stage in proceedings to determine whether the issue raised is insane or non-insane automatism, or whether the categorisation can be agreed with the other side.

- Do not forget that it may be appropriate to consider cases from other common law jurisdictions. In the case of sleepwalking, it may be worth looking to Canada and America. In the case of pre-menstrual syndrome, it may be helpful to consider the relatively recent decision in India.

- Don't be scared to make imaginative and principled arguments! We have seen that many of the cases are not clear-cut, and the law does not easily fit every scenario. The law is constantly developing, and in few areas is that clearer than in that of insane and non-insane automatism. Your case may be the one that results in further guidance and clarity for future defendants.

BIBLIOGRAPHY

Many thanks to the authors of the following works, whose writings provided assistance in the completion of this book.

- *Incapacity and Insanity: Do we Need the Insanity Defence?* R A Duff

- *Criminal Liability: Insanity and Automatism / A Discussion Paper* The Law Commission

- *Epilepsy and the Defence of Insanity – Time for a Change* Mackay and Reuber

- *PMS: Legal Usage and Limitations* Easteal and Kaye

- *The M'Naghten Rules – a brief historical note* McKay

- *Premenstrual Syndrome and Criminal Responsibility* Boorse

- *Criminal Law* Smith, Hogan & Ormerod

- *Text, Cases and Materials on Criminal Law* Ormerod & Laird

- *Diabetes Mellitus and Criminal Responsibility* Maher, Pearson and Frier

- *Violence, Sleepwalking and the Criminal Law* O'Ebrahim, Wilson, Marks and Peacock

MORE BOOKS BY LAW BRIEF PUBLISHING

A selection of our other titles available now:-

'A Practical Guide to Solicitor and Client Costs – 2nd Edition' by Robin Dunne
'Constructive Dismissal – Practice Pointers and Principles' by Benjimin Burgher
'A Practical Guide to Religion and Belief Discrimination Claims in the Workplace' by Kashif Ali
'A Practical Guide to the Law of Medical Treatment Decisions' by Ben Troke
'Fundamental Dishonesty and QOCS in Personal Injury Proceedings: Law and Practice' by Jake Rowley
'A Practical Guide to the Law in Relation to School Exclusions' by Charlotte Hadfield & Alice de Coverley
'A Practical Guide to Divorce for the Silver Separators' by Karin Walker
'The Right to be Forgotten – The Law and Practical Issues' by Melissa Stock
'A Practical Guide to Planning Law and Rights of Way in National Parks, the Broads and AONBs' by James Maurici QC, James Neill et al
'A Practical Guide to Election Law' by Tom Tabori
'A Practical Guide to the Law in Relation to Surrogacy' by Andrew Powell
'A Practical Guide to Claims Arising from Fatal Accidents – 2nd Edition' by James Patience
'A Practical Guide to the Ownership of Employee Inventions – From Entitlement to Compensation' by James Tumbridge & Ashley Roughton
'A Practical Guide to Asbestos Claims' by Jonathan Owen & Gareth McAloon
'A Practical Guide to Stamp Duty Land Tax in England and Northern Ireland' by Suzanne O'Hara
'A Practical Guide to the Law of Farming Partnerships' by Philip Whitcomb

'Covid-19, Homeworking and the Law – The Essential Guide to Employment and GDPR Issues' by Forbes Solicitors
'Covid-19, Force Majeure and Frustration of Contracts – The Essential Guide' by Keith Markham
'Covid-19 and Criminal Law – The Essential Guide' by Ramya Nagesh
'Covid-19 and Family Law in England and Wales – The Essential Guide' by Safda Mahmood
'A Practical Guide to the Law of Unlawful Eviction and Harassment – 2nd Edition' by Stephanie Lovegrove
'Covid-19, Residential Property, Equity Release and Enfranchisement – The Essential Guide' by Paul Sams and Louise Uphill
'Covid-19, Brexit and the Law of Commercial Leases – The Essential Guide' by Mark Shelton
'A Practical Guide to Costs in Personal Injury Claims – 2nd Edition' by Matthew Hoe
'A Practical Guide to the General Data Protection Regulation (GDPR) – 2nd Edition' by Keith Markham
'Ellis on Credit Hire – Sixth Edition' by Aidan Ellis & Tim Kevan
'A Practical Guide to Working with Litigants in Person and McKenzie Friends in Family Cases' by Stuart Barlow
'Protecting Unregistered Brands: A Practical Guide to the Law of Passing Off' by Lorna Brazell
'A Practical Guide to Secondary Liability and Joint Enterprise Post-Jogee' by Joanne Cecil & James Mehigan
'A Practical Guide to the Pre-Action RTA Claims Protocol for Personal Injury Lawyers' by Antonia Ford
'A Practical Guide to Neighbour Disputes and the Law' by Alexander Walsh
'A Practical Guide to Forfeiture of Leases' by Mark Shelton
'A Practical Guide to Coercive Control for Legal Practitioners and Victims' by Rachel Horman

'A Practical Guide to Rights Over Airspace and Subsoil' by Daniel Gatty
'Tackling Disclosure in the Criminal Courts – A Practitioner's Guide' by Narita Bahra QC & Don Ramble
'A Practical Guide to the Law of Driverless Cars – Second Edition' by Alex Glassbrook, Emma Northey & Scarlett Milligan
'A Practical Guide to TOLATA Claims' by Greg Williams
'Artificial Intelligence – The Practical Legal Issues' by John Buyers
'A Practical Guide to the Law of Prescription in Scotland' by Andrew Foyle
'A Practical Guide to the Construction and Rectification of Wills and Trust Instruments' by Edward Hewitt
'A Practical Guide to the Law of Bullying and Harassment in the Workplace' by Philip Hyland
'How to Be a Freelance Solicitor: A Practical Guide to the SRA-Regulated Freelance Solicitor Model' by Paul Bennett
'A Practical Guide to Prison Injury Claims' by Malcolm Johnson
'A Practical Guide to the Small Claims Track' by Dominic Bright
'A Practical Guide to Advising Clients at the Police Station' by Colin Stephen McKeown-Beaumont
'A Practical Guide to Antisocial Behaviour Injunctions' by Iain Wightwick
'Practical Mediation: A Guide for Mediators, Advocates, Advisers, Lawyers, and Students in Civil, Commercial, Business, Property, Workplace, and Employment Cases' by Jonathan Dingle with John Sephton
'The Mini-Pupillage Workbook' by David Boyle
'A Practical Guide to Crofting Law' by Brian Inkster
'A Practical Guide to Spousal Maintenance' by Liz Cowell
'A Practical Guide to the Law of Domain Names and Cybersquatting' by Andrew Clemson
'A Practical Guide to the Law of Gender Pay Gap Reporting' by Harini Iyengar

'A Practical Guide to the Rights of Grandparents in Children Proceedings' by Stuart Barlow
'NHS Whistleblowing and the Law' by Joseph England
'Employment Law and the Gig Economy' by Nigel Mackay & Annie Powell
'A Practical Guide to Noise Induced Hearing Loss (NIHL) Claims' by Andrew Mckie, Ian Skeate, Gareth McAloon
'An Introduction to Beauty Negligence Claims – A Practical Guide for the Personal Injury Practitioner' by Greg Almond
'Intercompany Agreements for Transfer Pricing Compliance' by Paul Sutton
'Zen and the Art of Mediation' by Martin Plowman
'A Practical Guide to the SRA Principles, Individual and Law Firm Codes of Conduct 2019 – What Every Law Firm Needs to Know' by Paul Bennett
'A Practical Guide to Adoption for Family Lawyers' by Graham Pegg
'A Practical Guide to Industrial Disease Claims' by Andrew Mckie & Ian Skeate
'A Practical Guide to Redundancy' by Philip Hyland
'A Practical Guide to Vicarious Liability' by Mariel Irvine
'A Practical Guide to Applications for Landlord's Consent and Variation of Leases' by Mark Shelton
'A Practical Guide to Relief from Sanctions Post-Mitchell and Denton' by Peter Causton
'A Practical Guide to Equity Release for Advisors' by Paul Sams
'A Practical Guide to the Law Relating to Food' by Ian Thomas
'A Practical Guide to Financial Services Claims' by Chris Hegarty
'The Law of Houses in Multiple Occupation: A Practical Guide to HMO Proceedings' by Julian Hunt
'A Practical Guide to Unlawful Eviction and Harassment' by Stephanie Lovegrove
'Occupiers, Highways and Defective Premises Claims: A Practical Guide Post-Jackson – 2nd Edition' by Andrew Mckie

'A Practical Guide to Financial Ombudsman Service Claims' by Adam Temple & Robert Scrivenor
'A Practical Guide to Advising Schools on Employment Law' by Jonathan Holden
'A Practical Guide to Running Housing Disrepair and Cavity Wall Claims: 2nd Edition' by Andrew Mckie & Ian Skeate
'A Practical Guide to Holiday Sickness Claims – 2nd Edition' by Andrew Mckie & Ian Skeate
'Arguments and Tactics for Personal Injury and Clinical Negligence Claims' by Dorian Williams
'A Practical Guide to Drone Law' by Rufus Ballaster, Andrew Firman, Eleanor Clot
'A Practical Guide to Compliance for Personal Injury Firms Working With Claims Management Companies' by Paul Bennett
'A Practical Guide to Dog Law for Owners and Others' by Andrea Pitt
'RTA Allegations of Fraud in a Post-Jackson Era: The Handbook – 2nd Edition' by Andrew Mckie
'RTA Personal Injury Claims: A Practical Guide Post-Jackson' by Andrew Mckie
'On Experts: CPR35 for Lawyers and Experts' by David Boyle
'An Introduction to Personal Injury Law' by David Boyle
'A Practical Guide to Subtle Brain Injury Claims' by Pankaj Madan

These books and more are available to order online direct from the publisher at www.lawbriefpublishing.com, where you can also read free sample chapters. For any queries, contact us on 0844 587 2383 or mail@lawbriefpublishing.com.

Our books are also usually in stock at www.amazon.co.uk with free next day delivery for Prime members, and at good legal bookshops such as Wildy & Sons.

We are regularly launching new books in our series of practical day-to-day practitioners' guides. Visit our website and join our free newsletter to be kept informed and to receive special offers, free chapters, etc.

You can also follow us on Twitter at www.twitter.com/lawbriefpub.